MW00476557

For Hannelore and Tatiana —

Blight

Beautiful, indispensable friends in my life — Ever —

April 4, 1995

Blight

a novel by

D. H. MELHEM

Illustrations by Christopher Maynard

Riverrun Press • *New York*
Calder Publications • *London*

BLIGHT

Copyright ©1994 by D.H. Melhem

Illustrations copyright ©1994 by Christopher Maynard

All rights reserved

This edition first published March 1995 by Riverrun Press, Inc., New York

Simultaneously published in Great Britain by Calder Publications Ltd., London

British Library Cataloging-in-Publication Data

Melhem, D.H.
Blight
I. Title II. Maynard, Christopher
823 [F]
ISBN 0-7145-4274-1

Library of Congress Cataloging-in-Publication Data

Melhem, D.H.
Blight: a novel/by D.H. Melhem;
illustrations by Christopher Maynard
p. cm.
ISBN 0-7145-4274-1
I. Title.
PS3563.E442B57 1995
813'.54—dc20

Book design by Dan Catalano

Manufactured in the United States of America

10 9 8 7 6 5 4 3 2 1

RPC

For my Mother and Father
For Tess, for Chester
For Claudia, who kept faith

Contents

Acknowledgments

Each leaf of this book is bound with the creative eye and heart of Richard Derus. It bears the imprimatur of the publisher I esteem the most.

Author's Preface

In this garden of our world, what may not arise from the uncherished soil? We reproduce as we are, not as we would be. The forms engendered, artifacts of isolation, prepare their indigenous ground without comrades, without love. The weak, the wavering, the small or strange—who will welcome them when they, too, are nourished by a tainted earth? In the reality of our dreams, the borders of value can meld and merge into chaos, into death. But we may intuit, from time to time, that loving necessity which, in its power, retains the communal edge.

Blight

I

Silence

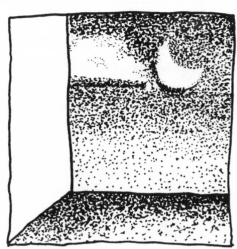

It had occurred to me that something was wrong in my garden. I had already thinned out the calendulas and zinnias; my tomato plants looked healthy and my cucumbers, squash, and potatoes had started out of the ground; but the row of giant phlox and salvia was barren.

Of course this was the first year I had tried either flower. Since my retirement five years ago, at the relatively young age of fifty-five (they had envied me at the paper mill, where I had endured thirty seemingly, at times, interminable years), I had come more and more to enjoy the rewards of gardening, both in physical exercise and edible produce. The flowers, also, pleased me greatly, with their beauty and their usefulness in attracting bees. My lawns are mostly clover, and bees do most of the work in setting the seeds, so you can see how I welcomed them.

I live alone. After my wife died, I had neither the will nor the need to continue working; my pension and savings adequately served my modest requirements. My son was married and living in California. He and his wife postponed their invitation until they got "settled." Eventually I lost my desire to travel there, or anywhere else for that matter. For everything there is a season. Years ago, before our son was born, I had wanted to go abroad with my wife Emma, but she thought it a waste of money when we should be preparing to become parents. A better life for one's child was her motto. So we didn't travel, except to her mother's house in Michigan, and then her mother died.

I had plenty of time to examine my life. It had become solitary, indeed, as if I were crafting it so, perfecting my isolation. A few neighbors stopped by when Emma died, but I discouraged their interest and after awhile there were no visits or calls. My son came in for the funeral and returned to California to be married. He sent a photograph of himself and his bride; I kept planning to frame it. When my television set broke, I remember feeling rage at another desertion (I couldn't help thinking of Emma's departure, like that of my son, as a willful act). I took the set to the dump. What need had I of the lacquered images of contented strangers who cared nothing about me? I reread books that I had purchased long ago. Franz Werfel's *The Forty Days of Musa Dagh* and John Steinbeck's *The Grapes of Wrath* were vaguely consoling. I could relate to people who had experienced losses. Occasionally I listened to the radio — but how much bad news could one absorb? Although my musical tastes were poorly developed (there had never been any music in my house as a child, and little enough to sing about there), once in awhile I listened to classical music. Most of it, however, made me quite sad and too intensely reflective. Eventually there was silence — sooner or later we all sit in that silent station by the window. Yet as the silence of nature took over, I could hear it more clearly as it swirled into the sounds of insects and birds and changing weather. The natural world approached until I could feel the weight of leaves pressing against the windows. The birds sang early and late; storms clattered about the house and shook the floorboards. Mostly it was quiet, and I tried to let the peaceable days pervade my spirit. Instead, I felt more and more the chill of stone. I thought of Emma in a nearby graveyard I no longer visited. With a peculiar detachment, I imagined my name, with various terminal dates, carved neatly beneath hers. What had it all meant? What had we meant to each other? In sickness and health. I had performed the duties expected, nursed her in her final illness. Now I was married to silence. Nevertheless, sometimes I could feel a rumbling, different from that of the probing thunder, a rumbling coming from the earth itself, as if it were getting ready to erupt.

Every morning I went out to look at my garden. Weeks passed, and still nothing appeared in the barren row. I debated plowing it up. Down on my hands and knees, like an animal at prayer, I would look. It was getting so late in the spring that I decided to turn the seeds under and plant something else. That Monday morning, I set out with my metal rake.

Outside the kitchen door the earth felt soggy and clung to my sandals. It had rained almost continuously for two days. The sky cleared above an immaculate air. I walked across the flagstone patio behind the house. If that row still appeared unproductive, my rake was ready.

But I was unprepared for my discovery. Around the back of the house and turning left to the garden, I saw a change. That row, that first row was no longer barren.

What was growing there — mushrooms? There are woods all around my land; mushrooms had often sprung up overnight, even on my lawn, so this seemed possible. I had, however, neither seen nor read of green mushrooms. Upon closer examination, I noticed that the thick stem of each plant was — how shall I put it — *notched*, as if indicating some rudimentary pattern. The caps were quite rounded, without gills, extending about an inch in diameter, approximately the width of the stems. In height, the plants were about six inches tall. There were ten plants.

I detected a new odor about the garden, and connected this odor with the strange plants. They bore no resemblance to any flowers with which I was familiar. Although I had never before planted phlox or salvia, I knew the flowers could not appear like this at any stage. And I had scattered a goodly number of seeds. Only ten plants of nearly identical height stood crowded together.

Odd as they were, their vigorous condition made me hesitate to destroy them. Perhaps they might bear some unusual flower or fruit. There was no need for haste. I could wait another day.

In the morning, I awakened to a rather pungent odor in my room. It was an unpleasant smell, reminiscent of a place I tried to recall, and then, yes, I remembered. It was a duck farm near a camp I had attended several summers as a child. With a start I threw back the cover and went to my window. Peering at the sunlit garden, I observed the singular plants. They had grown considerably overnight.

I grabbed my bathrobe, found a tape measure in a kitchen drawer, and hurried to the garden. The odor grew heavier as I approached. The plants themselves looked different.

They were changing color. The green had faded in spots to a kind of pale beige, almost a mushroom shade. The notches were deeper, the tops smaller in proportion to the girth of the stems. And each stem tapered and bulged into irregular contours.

I measured the plants. They had grown an average of two inches and now stood about eight inches tall. I examined the rest of my garden. A careful inspection disclosed what was happening. An army of minute, green insects had infested the flowers and were already devouring the first buds. The creatures were so numerous that many leaves seemed mobile and alive. A few insects had begun to attack the vegetables at the edge of the garden near the property line. Even there I noticed a dullness of tone and a torpid stance. It was true of them all: the cucumbers, squash, tomatoes, and potatoes. They had taken on the ambiguity of plants that ceased to grow. In great agitation, I ran to the house for my insect spray.

Several years before I had tried to garden organically. I fished with the main purpose of catching enough to enrich my compost pile. As a single person, I accumulated little garbage for this undertaking. I bought no insect sprays, resisting in advance the temptation to use them.

That first year, insect pests were absent. Everything grew nicely until late summer when the plants commenced to wilt and rot. A kind of fungus plagued them. Helplessly, I watched them die.

The next spring I had a very fine compost, all of which went into the garden. I had read somewhere that the treatment could cure almost any plant disease. I limed the soil which tended to be quite acid, and worked in some chicken manure for good measure. My pains were justified by a fantastic growth rate. By late July, the tomatoes bunched plentifully at the height of six-foot stakes.

Then it happened again.

One August morning last year, when the tomatoes were large and ripening heavily on the vines, with my squash and cucumbers nearly ready, the fungus appeared. A few patches of white, spongy growth, at first, which I removed from the soil, were replaced by a stubborn crust spreading more thickly until I could not remove it all. The leaves grew pale and turned brown with rot. I picked every tomato. Already some of the blossoms and buds had damped off. The squash and cucumbers were shriveling.

My nurseryman recommended a spray which I tested on a patch of fungus. The chemical worked. But the reprieve for the vegetables came too late. Abandoning theory, I determined to apply the spray early this year and did so, liberally and systematically. Until today, no fungus had reappeared. Yet the new blight was far deadlier.

I opened the kitchen door and hastened to the sink cabinet. Seizing an insecticide, I ran back to the garden and immediately sprayed the green bugs. They fell from the leaves, exposing the half-consumed, decaying remnants of healthy plants. I pressed down hard upon the nozzle of the spray can until the earth at my feet, teeming with the convulsions of countless bugs, grew still.

There was no satisfaction for me in the carnage. Although my garden was ruined, I allowed the strange plants to remain as curiosities. Promising neither beauty nor edibility, they alone grew unblighted, with a vigor that seemed to reinforce itself. In puzzlement and defeat, I left the garden.

I brewed six cups of coffee in my electric percolator (two cups for breakfast, two for lunch, one with dinner and one later). I always brewed six cups to save myself a repetitious effort. The quantity was unvarying; I expected no company nor solicited any. My usual four-minute egg poised in an egg cup on the table among two slices of toast, butter, strawberry jam, and a small glass of orange juice that always tasted a bit waxen from the container. I switched the radio on to hear the news, then snapped it off in the middle of a report on another wayward nuclear test.

How silent the house! I lived in a vast current of silence that carried me through the routines of my life. It was as if that life had been divided into one, enormous day through which I revolved, performing rituals detached from their significance. I wondered how things would have been—what I would have been—if my son had stayed.

But he had not, as I had not with my own parents, who now lay in a distant cemetery. He had rushed off to make his way in the world, thousands of miles from me.

I struggled to believe his leaving was a sign of his strength, something for which I could take a bit of credit. Must I blame myself for the loss of his affection? With Emma reciting the litany of our material needs, my son's needs, as I labored to progress and to advance my position from clerk to assistant vice-president, so that there was time at home only for meals and a newspaper and TV? Well, my boy had his mother! And I was tired. Used up.

There was no time for my son. I had worked to give him college, clothing, a car—the one he drove off in to California. When we did talk, I tried to make those occasions count. I taught him what I knew: that he needed cunning and egotism to get by. Otherwise, he would end up like me, struggling too hard for too little. Still he must have thought I was doing my thing, working like that. Was he merely selfish? Had I taught him too well? How could I change the world? He had to reconcile my practical instruction with his Sunday school lessons. That was his business, wasn't it? Don't we all separate the two in the apartheid of conventional morality? Anyway, Sunday school was Emma's idea. It probably just confused the boy.

After finishing my second cup of coffee, I put the dishes into the dishwasher and went outside to mow the lawn. I tossed a piece of bread to the towhee who always hovered nearby at that time. He ate it, then continued to thrash about in the dead leaves. I was pleased to see how this wild bird had gradually come to trust me. I wondered whether he would ever eat from my hand.

II

The Ground

The next morning I awakened to the same unpleasant odor. I went out quickly to see how the plants were doing and was greatly surprised at their height. Overnight, they had grown another two inches or so. The peculiar notches in the stems were more pronounced. In color, they were varied shades of beige; the green had quite disappeared. I decided to rake up the rest of the garden. The wilted plants and dead bugs depressed me.

The following morning it rained. From my bedroom window I saw that the plants had grown again considerably. There was no odor, perhaps because of the heavy downpour. I longed for the sight of a zinnia or two and resented the smooth, brown, empty face of the garden. I had done the job well. Nothing remained. Only the tall, parasitical plants developed. I suspected that these trespassers were taking such enormous nurture from the soil that nothing else could survive. I resolved to dig them up the next day.

Early the following morning I left the house, took the hoe which rested against the shingles near the back steps, and went determinedly to the garden.

The plants stood about twelve inches high. Once again they had grown approximately two inches.

Their form startled me. The bulge on either side of each stem was separating into paired, vertical appendages that started just below the caps and continued nearly to the middle of the stems. From midpoint to ground, the stems were dividing into two tapering stalks.

More curious to me, however, were the globular caps. How defined their notches had become, placed in identical patterns of two horizontal ones flanking a tiny, vertical bulge that protruded over a narrow slit. The total effect of the plants was undeniably that of rudimentary bodies.

My hesitancy returned. I began tentatively breaking ground in the adjacent furrow. Studying the first row, I noticed that the plant at the end was smaller than the rest. Still vacillating, I hoed close to it when, by accident or design, I struck the earth directly beneath so that it was raised and tilted.

Suddenly, the odor emanating from the plant (or plants) became intensely acrid and I dropped the hoe. Coughing and gagging, I backed away. The odor was everywhere. I panicked and fled.

Around the corner on the patio, the air was better. A chipmunk at the far end dashed off as I approached. The sun fell with impersonal cheer upon the house, the lawn, the trees where leaves rustled briefly now and then. Two bluejays drank from the birdbath at the perimeter of the lawn and flew off into the woods. Everything was as it had been.

Had imagination begun to rule me, as a result of my solitary ways? The bitter taste in my mouth was real. The foul air that clung to my throat was real.

Gripped by revulsion and fear, I sat immobilized on a chaise, pondering what to do. I decided to postpone any action until dusk.

To counter my growing anxiety, I took a long walk down to the bay. In the distant water, a group of swimmers called to each other, laughing. Sunlight held their bodies protectively in a dazzled ring. A few figures were scattered on the sand in angles of repose. I could have followed the seaweed tracings to the bathers. Perhaps there was someone to greet.

Instead, I moved in the opposite direction. Retreating from an invisible wall, I was immured within my own predicament. Only I knew what should be done, what I desired. Was there a difference?

As I passed the driftwood and the blooming rosa rugosa, it became clear that my interests lay in a return to tranquillity. The whole business had ceased to amuse, its novelty become sinister. One certainty held fast: no plants like these had ever existed.

If this were true, should I not call in a biologist, sharing my fantastic discovery? Were these plants mutants that even now might be undergoing change? What caused such phenomena, and why in my garden? I had read an article on radiation, how it altered the structure of cells. The erratic nuclear fallout reported on the radio was not the first such accident in past years. If the earth had been affected, was I affected also? No, I was healthy. I remained untouched.

Following my overriding impulse to withdraw from any potential social nuisance, I decided not to consult a scientist. It would be best for me simply to hoe under the plants and have done with the matter. Reaching the jetty, I felt hungry and started back for an early dinner.

At home my appetite gave way to a dread that the situation was eluding control. Perhaps someone should accompany me to the garden. My son would have done so. If I asked the neighbor down the road, a stranger, really, what reason could I give? A gardener might be summoned. To do what? Plow a narrow row of plants? Invite the hostile response I had suffered and broadcast the news? No, I had to do the job myself.

Outdoors, the day's brilliance had evaporated. I sought the hoe in its accustomed place near the door, and remembered leaving it in the garden. A breeze stirred the air. The back of my neck itched. My fingertips were cold as I scratched.

I made myself cross the patio briskly, then turned. Looking up from the grass to the garden, I could not take another step. The fear at the root of my imaginings had finally emerged. The plants were gone.

Against the foundation, like an ancient frieze, huddled ten small, thin—bodies, yes, bodies, I acknowledged in horror and relief, and they were imbued with an unmistakable vitality. The creatures seemed so terrified that I, equally frightened, made no sound. They were pale, mushroom-colored, their staring eyes the hue of mushroom gills. Their slow, convulsive clutchings were like the movements of newborn infants extending their arms, making fists, flexing their knees. Perfect, minute fingers; a suggestion of toes. These were adult bodies, however, thin, elongated, apparently sexless. I could distinguish no sign of hair.

As I gazed, my fear gave way to ludicrous images: a carnival sideshow, "Glabrous Guys and Gals" if they turned out to be male and female, or "Glabrous Ghouls" if they were neither. I pictured them holding a televised press conference, quizzed by leading scientists and reporters, with ensuing headlines: **NEW SPECIES UN-COVERED, EVOLUTION JUMPS FORWARD, EVOLUTION LEAPS BACKWARD**; a new "How-to" book, *Grow Your Own People*; national advertising campaigns by wigmakers showing them "before" and "after."

I laughed aloud. They started, and in a moment a whiff of that same, malevolent smell assailed me. I stepped back.

Yet I would have to speak, no matter how fearful they were. I had to know whether they could vocalize, as well as hear and see. Already I felt that we could communicate.

"Hello," I said softly.

They remained motionless. The odor, thank God, was not emitted.

I realized that to those small creatures I loomed a giant, threatening extinction. My height alone instilled mistrust. I sat down, changing my position as slowly as possible, watching them for any new evidence of alarm.

They trembled and drew closer together.

"Hello," I repeated. "Who are you? What are you doing here?"

They appeared to relax. The clutchings subsided. Bodily motions became defined, as if control and complexity were developing before my eyes. The "heap of life" separated into parts: two ventured a foot or so away from the rest. Deliberately, I extended my arms in a gesture of welcome. One creature took a wavering step toward me, then drew back into the group.

"Hello," I repeated.

At first I heard something like the gurgling coo of a pigeon, the sound growing and fluttering about them. I saw mouths open and close.

"Hello," I told them again.

All the mouths were moving now, and the sounds grew louder, clearer, until I distinguished a syllable: "lo." My God, I thought, they are imitating me!

"Lo, lo, lo," they said.

"Hello! Hello!" I insisted. "Hello!"

"Lo, alo, elo." Finally, one of them said, "Hello."

I was swept by a need to embrace that marvelous being, which, so lately out of the ground and off a stalk, could already mimic the complexity of sounds expressed in a single word. I must have started up, because the figures suddenly retreated.

I gave up the prospect of contact for the present and concentrated on building their trust.

A small fellow came forward.

"Hello." The clarity of his thin, piping tone startled me.

"How are you?" I asked.

"Ow are you?" he replied. He had reproduced the

sounds almost perfectly.

"My name is Joseph," I said, placing my palm upon my chest as I spoke the last word.

"My name is—Joseph," he answered. Had he hesitated, understanding that the word "Joseph" related to me?

He could have no concept of language, and a particular language at that. Not the way he had sprouted out of the ground. The creatures had grown like vegetables, right out of the soil. They were not visitors from another planet. I had watched them being formed in a womb of earth and air. They could hardly have brought actual knowledge with them from their source. Yet they held a further mystery. I would test them.

"What is your name?" I questioned.

A kind of smile moved the corners of his mouth. "What is your name?" he replied evenly.

I had the wild impression he was deceiving me in some way. But how could he know anything, anything at all? Possibly they were reading my mind. This notion appalled me so thoroughly that I felt an impulse to run, call the police, destroy them on the spot. If they could read my mind, however, they would know my intentions. And that knowledge would dispose them to concealment.

How was I to live with such monsters? I imagined myself in the house, transmitting my every wish and action to them outside. Would it be better to have them in the house where I might be able to lock them in a room?

Perhaps I victimized myself with suppositions. I was only guessing, after all. No matter how valid my conclusions, there were other premises. My own experience might be inadequate to deal with new facts. I must assume nothing and deal with appearances. Even if the creatures could read thoughts, or mine exclusively, I would try to believe what they wanted me to. Would they be put off by my guile?

I was being ridiculous. My concern with unlikely actions and reactions reflected fear, not fact. I would do what I must do.

Curiosity was the vehicle transporting me—where? And there was something else, a force propelling the wheels. Something profoundly exhilarating that I could glimpse now and then, like a figure in the sea. But what?

Endless analytic dissections: the icons of impotence. A man who thinks and thinks reasons deeds out of existence, like a prism shattering its light. A man of action is admired because he acts; his work is appraised by history. Had I not been such a man of this world, molded, judged, and judging by popular positions? The world had regarded me as a success—well, a near-success—and my family? My son?

The creatures took courage from my silence. They had moved as a group to within a few feet of me. I observed a "maleness" and a "femaleness" in that five had small, rounded bosoms, tantalizingly without nipples, which the other five did not. There were no genital organs apparent on any of them.

All the garden people were bald. And starkly naked. I imagined the females, especially, clothed, wearing wigs, and I thought they might be made nearly attractive.

Pointing to myself, I repeated slowly, "Joseph. Joseph."

One stepped closer and raised his arm.

"Joseph," he said. It was the bold fellow who had answered previously.

"I am Joseph," I persisted. "You are?"

"I am —." He paused, as if waiting for me to speak a name. I realized that I would have to name them. Numbers might be more appropriate! Or letters — Alpha, Beta, Gamma, etc. No, names would be more amusing, more human. But the creatures were not precisely human, were they? Adam and Eve? Better Edam and Ave. Edam, Ava. Those would do. Then Tom, Dick, and Harry. Why not? One more male: Isaiah, yes. Four more females: anything — Eenie, Meenie, Minie, and Moe. True, Moe was not very feminine. Neither were the other names, for that matter, but they were at least diminutive. Mona was better.

The speaker watched me patiently. I pointed at him. I said, "Edam. Edam."

Again his mouth made the funny smile I had noticed. Was he amused by me? "I am Edam." He had understood.

One by one they came to me. I bestowed each name with the solemnity of benediction; the image of a pope bobbed crazily in my mind. They moved so close that I could touch them, although I sensed the gesture would bring panic. Were their skins cool or clammy? Did they have bones? I could wring one of those slender necks like a fowl's. Without penalty. I wondered how and whether they would die.

This was not, however, my true interest, because I wanted them to live, and to live with me.

I rose carefully and walked slowly back to the house, half-expecting them to follow. Seated on the back steps,

I waited to see if they would. A few stars appeared faintly. Their numbers increased, charging the sky with brightness. Since I had no real desire to go into the house, I returned to the garden.

It was dark in that place and around it, dark and still, but I could feel a difference, an emptiness, actual, yet filled with a magic anticipation that thickened the air. A mosquito buzzed past me; the great white oak at the property line trembled its leaves. The ground people were gone.

Where?

I wandered about, treading with caution, to disturb no one, nothing that might be hiding there. Where could they be?

I took a few steps in every direction, and listened. All I heard was a faint chirping of birds. The sounds were unusual for this late hour. I could not identify the calls.

"Hello!" I said to the darkness. The chirping stopped.

"Hello! I am Joseph. Hello!"

Excitement might have deceived my senses. I thought I heard a tiny voice reply, "Hello," but I could not be certain. Real or imagined, the voice was succeeded by a chorus of bird twitterings, and then silence.

I do not know how long I stayed, calling and hoping for an answer. Despairing as I was, something in the darkness comforted me. The next morning, surely, they would be there.

III
Shelter

I slept poorly that night. Once I got up to check the locks on the windows and doors, twice to peer through the windows, from one side of the house and then another, and once to take three aspirins I hoped would quiet my nerves. I fell asleep for a few hours. At about seven o'clock I arose and went to my bedroom window. In the garden, nothing stirred.

Drawn by an impulse to rush out in search, held back by the prospect of disappointment, I proceeded with my usual day. Slowly I prepared and ate my customary breakfast. Finally, in a turmoil of reluctance and longing, I went to the garden.

They were gathered at the far corner of the foundation, beside a rabbit hutch I had built for my son's pet, one that had the ingenuity to escape as soon as it reached maturity. The flush of joy on my face must have been startling. The creatures regarded me with their pale, similar eyes. Quickly they seemed to relax while they examined the unpainted wooden structure.

The hutch resembled a miniature house without doors or windows. In size it was approximately one and a half feet high, three feet wide, and two feet deep. Several of the people climbed upon the roof. I was amazed at their agility and speed, and at the temerity they now displayed in my presence.

Edam stood by the doorway, his eyes focused on the interior. He glanced at me as if to make sure that I maintained my distance, then darted inside. The others clustered about the opening, twittering and humming like a congregation of birds and bees whose language, undoubtedly, they had acquired. It was the language I had heard the night before. After a minute or two Edam emerged and motioned to one of the females who might have been his "Ava." She followed him in. The rest continued their bustling commentary, heedless of my presence.

This new attitude perplexed me more than their original suspicion. Dullness could not account for the change. In physical sensitivity and intelligence, they were precocious. The explanation might be their adaptability, which apparently exceeded that of human beings. But was it not intelligence, in which cunning shared, that made for adaptability? Or was intelligence itself transmuted and refined by these beings into a new dimension of perceiving? Could they already know I meant them no harm?

Edam reappeared, with Ava behind him. This time he stood in the doorway, motioning away the others, shouting what must have been commands. He sounded like the blue jays that screamed and played about the bird bath. The rest withdrew, still twittering and humming, but in a different tone. As Edam stepped forward, his voice dropped to a chirp, which alternated with an insinuating coo.

One by one the group entered the hutch for a short tour of inspection. Outside, they surrounded Edam who chattered earnestly while pointing to the pile of stakes and lumber that lay nearby. They ran to the lumber with which I had intended to fence in some of my property. Pausing there, they looked at me quizzically. Still wary, I neither spoke nor moved, giving them instead a broad smile of approval. In pairs, they lifted the strips of wood and leaned them at about a forty-five degree angle against the lower shingles of my house. In proportion to their size, the strength of the creatures impressed me. They hurried back and forth until they had erected a lean-to. It extended from the rabbit hutch to a spot behind the board fence which continued the façade of my house to the left and was covered with climbing roses.

Edam assisted his comrades, bearing the weight near the center of each strip, sounding and gesturing constantly, standing back to appraise the work, and issuing further directions. The smallest male, whom I had named Tom, appeared playfully at ease, delightedly poking three of the females whenever he passed them. The first one, Eenie, a rather squat female, responded to these attentions with much animation, which I assumed to be pleasure. She blinked her lashless lids at him, advancing and retreating coquettishly.

Meenie, similar in stature to Eenie but quite spare, took interest in both Eenie and Tom, dividing her time between them. Minie, who was slightly taller than Eenie

and Meenie, seemed distressed by Tom's pranks. Once
when Tom poked her she ran to the tall male I had named
Dick. As she twittered, he smiled and uttered a little,
human-sounding laugh, the first I had noted from any of
them. Had he "learned" my laugh? Was it a recognition
of humor?

Of the rest, Harry, well-shaped, tall, struck me as the
most withdrawn. Several times I saw him standing aside,
watching Ava. Isaiah was aptly named, I mused. He bab-
bled and scampered to and fro with the commitment of a
prophet, commented on each activity or the lack of it, on
the conduct of the enterprise and those involved. He was
slightly thinner and shorter than the others; his rather
querulous voice conveyed the impression of a cranky old
man. Mona, frail and nearly formless, bustled about
Isaiah. She chirped and scolded, vacillating between filial
obsession and fishwifely abuse.

Of all the people, Ava intrigued me the most. She was
the largest female, the best-proportioned, the most
human-looking. The others were more sleek and flat-
hipped; Ava was full-bosomed and heavy-hipped.
Curiously, the longer I observed her and her little world,
the larger everyone seemed, as if we were approaching
each other's size.

I wondered how Ava—or any of her peers, for that
matter—would be to the touch. Soft? Spongy, like the
mushrooms they resembled? Could they reproduce? If
so, how? Were their feelings and responses like mine?
Above all, what did they think of me?

With a twig, Edam marked a line on the soil where the
boards rested. Tom, Dick, Harry, and Isaiah dug along the

line with bits of wood, making slow progress. The females gathered around the workers, encouraging them and helping to move the dirt away from the diggers. At first the new labors puzzled me. I watched Edam lowering the end of a strip into place. He had invented a way to secure the shelter; the trench was designed to hold it in the ground.

It had always pleased me to work with my hands—a release, permanent now, from the tedious paperwork at the paper mill—so I seized the chance to demonstrate my good will. Although I rose in slow motion, they promptly halted their activity, like children playing "statues." From the toolshed a few yards away, I glanced at the static figures. Retrieving a shovel and a trowel, I hastened back.

Armed with the large shovel in one hand and the knife-shaped trowel in the other, I must have presented a menacing sight. Suddenly, a fierce gust of the nauseating odor I had smelled before shot at me. I dropped the tools and fell to the ground, choking and retching. When the air cleared, I saw myself completely encircled, a Gulliver among Lilliputians.

Had they leveled me to their physical plane in order to deal with me? When they stepped on the grass, so close to my body I could grasp them, they did no further harm. They retained their weapon and had demonstrated its effectiveness. And they could use it at will.

But they could not read my mind. That was a consoling thought. If they had read my intention to assist them with the trench, they would not have reacted defensively. Or were they mischievous? Testing their strength? Able to receive visual impressions more quickly than psychic ones? There was an even more disquieting possibility.

Perhaps they had acted to conceal their remarkable pow-
ers and literally put me off the scent.

My head ached more with conflict than assault. My
habit of suspicion and mistrust was too deeply ingrained,
casting theory after theory to destroy the pleasure I
might take in the creatures. Again I resolved to be scien-
tific, businesslike, confining myself to facts. I would keep
a notebook, an account of events.

Edam stood temptingly at my right hand. He studied
my hand and my face while his voluble companions
marched around me. Abruptly he strode away. A moment
later, he reappeared, carrying an object with both hands.
It was my trowel. He placed the handle in my out-
stretched right hand. "Joseph," he said quietly. The
utterance sounded friendly, even apologetic.

I grasped the trowel by its handle and sat up. The
others drew excitedly to one side, near Edam. I found my
shovel, picked it up with my left hand, and stood erect.
To my relief, nothing happened. I walked toward the
lean-to; my companions accompanied me at a distance.
When I reached it they stopped, also, a few yards away,
as if waiting to see what I would do.

I picked up my sturdy shovel and began to deepen their
trench. The job quickly accomplished, I used my trowel to
even the depth of the furrow. My meticulous nature
impelled me to do the work as well as I could. I nailed two
supports to the strips, one across the top and one at the bot-
tom, to hold them securely. Gingerly I trod back to the tool
shed and selected a hammer and some nails.

As I began to hammer, the twitterings became more
rapid and audible. The people were now a yard or so

away, flanking me. My pounding sent them into flurries
of response to each driven nail.

When the shelter was ready, I raised it and lowered
one side into the trench. I rested the top against the low-
est shingle of the house, moving it upward into a tight
wedge beneath the bottom edge of the second shingle. To
all appearances, the task was finished.

My pause triggered a celebration. The people jumped
gleefully and dashed back and forth through the shelter.
Their approval filled me with pride. I knew, however,
that a strong wind could blow the structure away. The
trench had to be filled with stones and sand to hold the
wood. My nerves had worn me to the verge of exhaus-
tion. More important, I believed that cooperation would
launch a friendly relationship. Thus I decided to enlist
their help.

I found a few stones of various sizes which I held out
to them, repeating, "Stone. Stone," before casting them
into the trench. I resumed gathering stones, repeating the
word as I dropped them in.

The creatures ran toward the woods, then returned in
haste. Each bore one or two stones, depending upon the
size. At the edge of the trench they looked inquiringly at
me, and I heard a murmured repetition of the word
"stone." Making no effort to relieve them of their loads, I
smiled and indicated the depression. They understood I
wanted them to drop the stones there, for they did so. I
too continued to collect stones; the work had become a
game. There was much twittering and poking of the
females by the males. The whole undertaking was
achieved with dispatch and good cheer.

When we had amassed a surplus of stones, I hesitated to stop the activity, but at last raised my hands, saying, "No more stones." They understood and gathered beside me. I covered the stones liberally with sand. Then I stepped around the rose fence and crossed the front lawn to the side of the house where I kept the garden hose. The nozzle was already attached. I took the lariat of hose off the hook, unwinding the green tubing behind me as I neared the garden.

Afraid that the new apparatus trailing my reappearance might frighten them again, I walked slowly toward the group. How delightful it was to find them merely curious. I rotated the nozzle, directing a stream of water on the sand in the furrow. Certain that it was firmly packed among the stones, I turned off the water, shoveled in the remaining sand and earth, and tamped them down against the wood with the back of my shovel. Now concerned with the top of the boards, I hammered three long nails at a slightly declining angle through the wood and into the shingle. At last I stood back to view my work. The task was well done.

As if sharing my satisfaction, the creatures crowded around me, crying, "Joseph! Joseph!" in a kind of chanting praise. They ran through their new house and about my legs. For the first time, their tiny hands brushed my calves. The touches, like sparks, filled me with elation. No longer was I feared. And so I sat down.

This time my presence on the ground drew them to me, to touch my hands, climb over my legs, timidly, yet with a growing exuberance and abandon, recalling their prancing joy over the shelter. I was swept by a desire to pick up one of them, particularly Ava, but decided, judiciously, first to try one of the males. Edam appeared to be the most intrepid, and nearest to my hand which fascinated him, probably because of its size. With a smile fixed upon my face, presenting as casual a demeanor as I could, I grasped him gently about the waist and raised him to my eye level.

His lightness startled me, as if he were hollow. His skin felt extremely smooth and cool to the touch. Giving no sign of alarm or hint of struggle, he relaxed in my hand like one who had expected, even wished for my move. With difficulty, I contained my enthusiasm. I wanted to shout something—"Hooray!" or "Eureka!"— but dreaded arousing alarm. So I smiled again and said, "Hello, Edam."

I was beside myself with happiness at his reply, because it showed his intelligence and comprehension and convinced me that the ground people could learn my language within a very short time.

"Hello, Joseph," he said.

IV

Friends

Guided by my son's old grammar, I spent the next few days instructing my companions in language. They absorbed and retained information; their reasoning was acute. Their grasp of verbal syntax showed ease with logical inference; their immediate comprehension functioned almost like memory.

Those were happy days for me. In the mornings we strolled through my property. Along the way, I identified trees, berry bushes, insects, everything we could see and hear, touch or smell, and they repeated the words in their clear, high voices. The wooded areas behind and on either side of the house, and beyond the front lawn, gave us total privacy. Near the road (rarely used except by the truck of an unseen postman on his daily rounds—even junk mail was rarely deposited in my mailbox), a rocky embankment on which my wife had vainly tried to cultivate a garden of succulent plants declined steeply. Across the road lay the ample woods of a reclusive neighbor who was absent most of the year. Nobody intruded on my life anymore. There was just me—and the creatures.

What sustained them? I had never seen them consume anything. How were they being nourished? Except for their eyes, mouths, and pinhole-sized hearing apertures, I observed no bodily openings. Their "noses" were minuscule protrusions below their eyes. Possibly orifices existed between their legs and became visible only upon excitation or when functioning. On the other hand if my observations were correct regarding their nether areas, that would explain the lack of ordinary food requirements, since no waste passages would be needed.

I wondered whether these beings could procreate in any way or have some kind of sexual gratification. At the time we were building the shelter, I had noticed a sort of male-female response, a bantering contact apparently not exchanged between the males. As I came to know them, I watched Tom share most of his leisure time among Eenie, Meenie, and Minie who regularly fled his presence. She usually managed to alight near Dick, who would put his hand over hers protectively.

Mona persisted in her role as acolyte to Isaiah. It was difficult to determine whether he welcomed or merely endured her ministrations. Nevertheless, he never motioned her away. Even Harry in his tall, cool, enigmatic presence seemed always to be standing aside, waiting, stalking someone. He would stare at Ava from time to time; she was the object of his interest.

Ava enjoyed every attention shown her, from whatever source. Poised and beautifully shaped as she was, I interpreted her actions as typically feminine. Self-contained, she showed a gracious concern for all who addressed her, as she turned upon each speaker, including me, her sweet, level, even sympathetic gaze. Then her mood would shift so that her movements became voluptuous and inviting. If the adjective were not laughable, I would say she was, at least potentially, a woman on the grand scale.

Ava was much admired by the males, yet I had never seen anyone touch her but Edam. He was not overtly affectionate, treating her with a laconic possessiveness. He himself was a being of obvious force. No one trespassed on the rights he asserted. That first morning, before the shelter was built, he had declared himself boldly about the rabbit hutch. I assumed that he and Ava used it at night. Never having seen any of the creatures sleeping, I guessed that the others used the new quarters, while the hutch belonged exclusively to their leader and his mate.

No one ever challenged Edam. While I could admire, to an extent, his bold rapacity, his manner irritated me. It would be silly to say I envied him, which would make as much sense as being jealous of a bird or a fish. What did he have that I wanted? I could lift and handle each of the ground people whenever I wished, though not to the degree I might have preferred. This power, I still believed, represented the tangible superiority of my position. Yet Edam's control troubled me. Why?

A sense of order, a flair for organization, had always been my forte. I should therefore have enjoyed Edam's leadership for its own sake. His role as chief facilitated my dealings with his people, yet his very "chiefness" unsettled me. Maybe this experience should have been a dream in which I, the dreamer, could gratify my needs with impunity; where the conflict between Edam and me, veiled within a context of wish-fulfillment, would signify no more than amoral self-interest. But Edam was real. He was a moral as well as a physical entity.

Why did only an imaginary situation transcend good and evil? The needs of the body, the self, eluded the artifice of morality. Surely my business years at the paper mill had taught me this, and I had practiced it willingly. I would not fall into the trap set for the feckless and gullible, baited with pity and fear by those no better than myself.

Fortified by my realistic view, I no longer worried about the creatures' extra-sensory capabilities. Because they were so sensitive to me, however, it would be politic to disguise my feelings, particularly toward Edam. Even more, by actually thinking the opposite, I would make pretense into self-protection. I strove to think favorably of Edam and nearly convinced myself that my admiration was not false.

One morning in the garden, when I was seated in their midst, conducting a language lesson, my pupils suddenly began to shriek as they rushed pell-mell after Edam into the rabbit hutch. Crowded, they must nevertheless have understood it to be the safest place, since the opening was small and could be protected. A short distance away on the grass poised the object of their terror: an inquisitive, fat squirrel. It surprised me that these products of nature would be frightened by an ordinary animal, of a type they must have grown with. I resolved to buy some chicken wire that afternoon and fence in the entire garden.

The group's flight into the hutch revealed, however, their need for an enclosed shelter. I planned to buy them lumber and nails, toy-sized hammers, saws, screwdrivers and pliers, hinges and knobs, to teach them the use of each for our mutual benefit and diversion. That afternoon I drove into the village and bought enough chicken wire to protect the entire garden. I found the necessary tools at the hardware store and stopped at the lumber yard, where I bought some wood. Upon my return, I took my purchases to the garden and lay them out, explaining the purpose I had in mind.

The people seemed very pleased. They lifted the corners of their mouths in that special smile which made me smile all the more. They were quite taken with the tools and congregated about them, running their hands over the surfaces. I raised each instrument in turn, demonstrating its proper grasp and usage and invited them to do the same. Edam made the first attempts, holding the tools with both hands as I had done, since I saw that their fingers barely fit around the handles. The rest imitated the procedures. I was impressed by their strength and precision, particularly in sawing and hammering nails.

I proposed triangular doors to fit either end of the shelter and temporarily placed the hinges and drawer-knobs on the separate pieces, to illustrate the effect. Everyone was excited and clambered over the board like exuberant children. I indicated the path of the saw and began a stroke into the lumber. My lesson was superfluous.

When I put down the tool and the wood, Edam chattered directions to the others. They brought over a short plank on to which they lifted an end of one board. Edam took the saw with both hands, walked up the slight incline and, kneeling at the edge, began carefully to saw. Pausing, he instructed his comrades. In a few minutes, Harry was similarly engaged, sawing with effort, accurately. The rest solicitously watched the pair, whose competence left me at ease to begin frames for the new doors.

As I worked, it struck me that the rabbit hutch also needed a door. I worried about Ava being nibbled by a chipmunk or squirrel or even a vagrant rabbit. Seated beside the shelter and absorbed in finishing the first frame, I was startled to hear Edam's voice.

"Joseph," he said, standing next to my foot. It felt as if my calf were speaking. "Have you finished sawing?" I asked.

"Yes."

"Good."

"Good," he agreed. Was he mocking me?

I was impatient to finish my own task. "What do you want?"

"A door," he answered.

"You mean for the hutch—I was just thinking of that." Childishly, I had wished the suggestion to be my own. He was welcome to do the work.

The corners of his mouth rose in that tiny half-smile. "I will make it now," he announced. Did his words reflect linguistic awkwardness or increasing arrogance? There was no indication of a request. They all had understood the difference between "shall" and "will," "may I" and "can I" and the requirements of courtesy, which they interpreted as a kind of password game. Edam was simply telling me what he would do.

"Go right ahead," I said.

"Give me that." He indicated the pencil with which I had outlined the doors. My annoyance bubbled over.

"You must say 'Please give me.' It's the way we speak."

"Please give me," he repeated, continuing to smile. I gave him the pencil. He took the wood through the arched doorway of the hutch, called Isaiah inside to support it against the opening, and traced the outline from outside. I appreciated his cleverness and spunk. There was something admirable about him. In spite of difficulty sawing along the curve, he never once asked for help and stopped only when he had finished the task.

At last the three doors were set upon their hinges and their knobs attached. Everyone was intrigued by the act of opening and closing. The shelter provided the most fun. They could open one door, run straight through and exit by the other. The construction permitted freedom of movement. Their satisfaction justified my design, and I was pleased.

For the time being I could abandon the chicken wire project. I set the roll by the patio fence, under the eaves. That night I slept soundly, convinced that our common efforts had achieved harmony.

V
Visit

The idea of their visiting my house kept recurring, but I did not mention it. I still feared them somewhat, remembering their potency. Indoors they could attack swiftly, lock me in my room when I was too weak to escape. As the days passed, I thought the invitation might frighten them, and I mused on whether they might indeed have cause to be afraid. Lately I had felt mild urges to seize them, put them into my house and keep them there. Although I dared not forcibly impose my will, my hopes kept rising.

Disquieting thoughts would follow. Their possible sensitivity to weather changes troubled me. We had had little rain until now, the end of August. Next month promised heavy rains and a cooler season. After that, frost. I was content that the shelters could withstand both wind and rain; the creatures must be able to cope with the elements, even if deprived of their dwellings, unless "humanizing" had lessened their adaptation to the environment. The prospect of freezing temperatures and snow bothered me more keenly. If the ground people found the weather increasingly harsh, however, their intelligence would lead them indoors. They must first be made aware of the house as an alternative.

On a cloudy day I proposed the visit; the weather bureau had predicted a storm by evening. As usual, I sat among my friends in the garden and offered my invitation as an educational journey. I had taught them about outdoor phenomena and now proposed that they investigate the house as well. They glanced at each other, seeming to agree to this reasonable proposal. They accompanied me to the back door. Once there, however, they became shy. I entered first and held the door open. They murmured in hesitation. Edam and Ava entered, ushering in the others.

I should have taken them in the front way, but it was a door I hardly ever used. Their first impression must have been awesome: the kitchen, with its array of gigantic white machines. I set the stool near the counter so they might feel free to climb and examine whatever they wished. I asked permission to hold them up, and did so in pairs so that each might see the surfaces of machines and the counter and the dishes, glassware, and foodstuffs in the cabinets. As I did so, I remembered how I used to hold my son on my shoulder at parades. I named each object I touched; they needed no repetitions.

When I opened the refrigerator door, everyone drew back with a shiver. I explained the purpose of its temperature and described the items revealed. Not much was there: left-over chicken, a container of milk, prune juice, four oranges, an apple, cheese, three eggs, butter, strawberry jam; but more lay in the freezer: frozen dinners, fish, meat, ice cream, two pies. I tried to stock up occasionally so that I could avoid frequent marketing in town. None of the visitors had seen me eat; perhaps they supposed that I was self-sustaining, like them. If they were repelled by the thought of my chewing a fowl or fruit (they had already observed birds and animals consume worms, insects, and nuts), they kept their feelings to themselves.

My house was small: a dining area which I seldom used, preferring to eat in the kitchen; a quietly furnished, Early American-style living room, with an austere landscape over the fireplace, a Yankee Clipper ship model that had been in my mother-in-law's family, and a commode above which rested a framed sampler reading "God Bless Our Home." Emma had bought that at her church fair when we were first married. There were three bedrooms and one bathroom.

In the living room I paused at each article, so that my peripatetic lesson might disclose the furnishings, colors, textures of my world. When I opened books, I saw how easily the group would read. I imagined educating them with worthy literature, so that we might hold discussions on nippy evenings around the fire. They were fascinated by the fireplace. I lit a piece of paper with a match and threw it in. The flame briefly reflected the yellow glints in their eyes. Ten pairs of strangely luminous orbs spanned the hearth.

My room delighted them the most. They were enthralled by my closet, the assortment of jackets and slacks, workshirts and shorts, the enormous shoes and sneakers on the floor. They marveled at the lower drawers of my bureau and requested me to pull out each one and place it on the floor for their scrutiny. Lining up around the rim, they reached in to handle my pajamas and briefs. Edam climbed in to march across the fabrics that billowed about him. I removed several items to the floor. The females were especially taken with an old pair of rayon pajamas upon which they sat. Ava held up a hem of the fabric against her body as she stroked the material.

I moved the standing mirror from atop the chest and set it before her on the floor. She seemed enchanted with her image and fondly patted the glass. The others soon crowded her aside. Their struttings and preoccupation with the mirror indicated that their curiosity might be laced with vanity. To their audible disappointment, I removed the glass and, to distract them, replaced it with a small top drawer filled with my socks. Tom was the first to step into one with both legs. Holding the top under his arms, he hopped about as in a sack, to the giggles of the others who did the same. After I unballed more pairs so that all could participate, I laughed at the ten animated socks bobbing around the room. They did not tire of the activity and seemed unaware of me.

I brought my palms together sharply. "Please. Enough for now." Although startled by my voice and clapping, the merrymakers were loath to relinquish the socks. "I must put things away now," I added, picking up the drawer.

They relinquished the hose which I promptly crammed inside. My back ached from crouching and bending and lifting drawers. I told them I needed to lie down and stretch out. Pulling back the covers, I climbed in, partly to demonstrate how I slept at night, mostly to rest a few minutes. My head scarcely had dented the pillow when everyone scurried up the thin bedspread, under the sheet and out again and over my encased figure. They were so light that their weight through the covers felt like a tickling. A few who had boldly crawled under the bedclothes increased the sensation with their probing, and I laughed.

I groped beside me where I had seen Ava dive beneath the sheet. Grabbing a smooth little body, I lifted it out. Ava, smiling at me. My pleasure sent a peculiar tingling down my spine and around my groin as my shirt grew damp. I moved my thumb delicately over her tipless breasts. Her expression did not change. I felt—desire. Lost within astonishing urgencies, I did not hear the crescendo of grumbling. My guests were standing on the bed near my pillow. "Let her go!" voices shouted into my ear. "Let her go!"

I jerked up my knee to camouflage my unexpected reaction. "She is perfectly free to go," I muttered defensively, setting her down.

"Joseph is a good man!" she rebuked the others. Edam, glaring, took her roughly by the arm. One by one the visitors descended from the bed.

I felt mortified. As I left the room and watched them standing in the doorway, I realized that my indiscretion had revived their fear. Yet the experience held a surprising compensation. I recalled what Ava had said in her sweet, piping voice. Her kindness and naïve acceptance of me were even more appealing than her voluptuousness.

How defenseless and yielding she seemed. I was thinking about her too much.

"I am your friend," I assured the group. "I would not hurt any of you. Ava knows I meant her no harm. Have I done anything but help you? Just what," I questioned boldly, "did you think I was doing?"

No one spoke. Then Harry and Dick approached Edam. "He helped us," I heard them say. The three conversed in their bird language, joined by the others. I caught Ava's words to Edam. "He did not harm me." Facing general agreement on my innocence, Edam relented. "Let us see the rest of your house," he said gruffly.

In subdued spirits we resumed the tour. The garden people were as disinclined to see any more bedrooms as I was to show them. The bathroom, however, stirred their interest. I set the creatures down at the far end of the tub. Following Edam, they dashed forward and back through the gentle spray. They chattered and called to each other, "Rain!"

Their happy chirping indicated a trust restored. Yet seeing them in the tub reveived my own fear. Had they wrecked my sanity? I could turn up the hot water, whose temperature was set at a suitably scalding degree. Two quick rotations and I could end them. But somehow that would also be the end of me.

They were asking to leave the tub. I turned off the water and put them on the bathmat. Of course they were dripping wet, soaking the mat. I took washcloths from the linen closet and offered them as towels. Ava and Minie accepted; the others refused and simply jumped up and down, drying off as the water droplets easily glided from their bodies.

"What is that?" asked Tom, pointing to the toilet. I explained the formation of waste products as simply as I could. It embarrassed me to do so, especially to creatures apparently without gross bodily functions.

"If you kill something with your mouth," said Isaiah, "your body throws away what you cannot use."

His version made me uncomfortable. "That is a way of looking at it. But everything—most things" (I thought of the many live clams I had eaten) "are dead when I eat them, since even clams," I confessed (they had seen clam shells in the garden), "have no feelings as we understand them."

"As the clams understand them?" he persisted. Uncertain whether Isaiah was questioning or being critical, and sensing an ambivalence in his words, I let the matter drop and absent-mindedly flushed the toilet. Everyone rushed out, afraid of the clamor. I apologized for causing alarm. That a flick of my finger could shoot something down through pipes to an omnivorous death tank horrified them. Perhaps they imagined themselves making the dreadful trip, being disposed of in the same way.

To divert their attention, I opened the door to the linen closet next to the bathroom. They found the care of my body an oddly complex and redundant ritual. Some were enchanted by the oval, mildly fragrant cakes of soap, so wet and soft at the sink, so hard and dry here they could be spun on the wooden floor.

"What is in there?" asked Edam, pointing to the next closet. I was a trifle diffident. Inside, my fishing rods stood like javelins. Even as I mentioned their use, I already saw them from another perspective.

"The fish is alive when you take it from the water?" queried Edam.

"Yes."

"It has not attacked you."

"No—usually. No." (I thought of sharks, of a barracuda that I had heard of on the radio, jumping into a fishing boat and attacking a fisherman. Was that self-defense on the part of the fish? Vengeance?)

"And then it dies when you eat it."

"No. Before."

"You kill it."

"Not precisely. It dies because it has left the water."

"Taking it from its home kills it."

I didn't like this inquisition. "Yes."

"You kill it," he insisted. Edam was downright obnoxious, but I kept silent. "You kill it and burn it and eat it," he went on. "Then you throw away what you do not use—in there." He pointed to the bathroom.

His disgusting interpretation would surely damage my status with his companions, who regarded me quizzically. "We are different creatures," I told him, suppressing my anger. "We have different needs. You do not have to eat to live. I do. If it is bad to eat, then it is bad to live. But I say that it is good for me to live and for you to live, even though we are different." My words had some effect; I heard a reassuring sort of humming and muttering.

Edam smiled. "You fish because you are hungry."

"Yes."

"Do you always eat the fish?"

"Sometimes I put them into the ground, so they can decay and feed the plants."

"Then you do not like to kill the fish."

"Of course not!"

"Do you like to catch the fish?"

Where was he taking me? "I usually like to catch fish. It is considered a sport."

"When you catch them they die. It does not surprise you that they die. You know they will."

He had trapped me. I refused to reply.

"You like to catch them and you know they will die. Then do you not like to kill the fish?" His smile was triumphant. I fancied reeling him out of the water, thrashing, tugging vainly at the large hook tearing his mouth.

"I do not like to kill anything," I answered coolly and shut the door, ending the dialogue.

"Friend Joseph," remarked Harry in a kindly tone, "in the morning I have seen the robin. He pulls a worm out of its home in the ground. He eats. He shares with his nest. Then he drops from his tail what he does not need. The bird does no harm. His worm is like your fish." Harry smiled. His analogy, though leveling, was true to his perception and intention to support me. I valued this support, not only for its timeliness but also for the future when I might need an ally.

Edam's view, which placed me in the category of predatory birds and animals, I objected to most bitterly. Did the ground people consider themselves a superior moral species, they who had attacked me so wantonly with their peculiar weapon? The ten creatures were not even human! They did not eat or drink or clothe themselves or behave as members of my species. They were entirely different from me. I sank my reproaches as far back into my consciousness as they would go. "Thank you, Harry," I said, letting the matter rest.

Still anticipating a time when the ground people might live indoors, I invited them to visit the cellar. It was my hope that its privacy and space, even its dampness, would appeal to them. Like the upstairs, the walls were painted white, but the floor had not been finished. The time to do that was long past. Emma had wanted us to tile the floor right away, but there was the mortgage, the expenses of parenthood, schools, and later on, her illness. Years of that. Bit by bit one lost the knack of living.

I peered ahead to the discarded yet usable furniture: a rattan sofa and chairs, which had been replaced on my patio with a more weather-resistant aluminum set. Down the cellar steps all followed me, dropping gracefully from one tread to the next in a sort of dance. At the bottom they scattered to explore corners and objects. While I rejoiced in their enthusiasm, I tempered my pleasure with discretion, having learned my lesson upstairs. Offhandedly I stated that they were welcome to return to the cellar whenever they wished for however long they cared to stay.

While my general invitation was sincere, I felt my interest gathering me into a strange current, drawing me toward an obscure destination that somehow involved Ava. I thought of her little body on the bed, a bald, undressed doll. I dared not single her out again. Would I ever be able to? With her peers I needed constantly to ingratiate myself, a condition for which I held Edam primarily responsible.

After naming and explaining the items in the cellar — paints, tools, canned goods and sundry supplies (some of them forgotten) that I stored downstairs—I sat on a low step, watching the tourists. Their curiosity never lagged. Edam climbed from one open shelf to another; Dick and Minie followed him. Isaiah started to copy them, but Mona pulled him back, insisting he play with her. She had found a small, dead tennis ball (my son's) and gleefully rolled it to Isaiah who glumly rolled it back. Harry chased Ava around a post.

When I glanced at a corner of the sofa, it had become a tangle of arms and legs moving languidly and rhythmically like a pale, shapely octopus that turned out to be Tom, Eenie, and Meenie. Though I doubted their ability to go past superficial caresses, I believed that the trio's wantonness should have been carried on in private. I might well be a stuffy leftover from another time; nevertheless, their actions reinforced my feeling of superiority. Devoid of any modesty, the creatures were behaving on a sub-human level. One could observe them with no more compunction than one would have examining frogs in a laboratory, mere scientific data.

Harry was playing his pursuit game in earnest. I spotted Edam across the room, climbing to the highest shelf. Harry and Ava ran faster and faster around the post. He caught her arm. She broke free and ran to me, flinging herself at my feet. Her pursuer took a few steps after her and paused sheepishly.

"I do not like the game," she told me emphatically. I gently stroked her head. "Harry hurt me." She lifted her hand in evidence. I saw no mark.

"I think he likes you," I said.

"He is a silly thing."

Her use of the noun made me uneasy. Did she regard the other creatures as objects or assume this was my opinion? Mistrust again confounded me. Ava's language was limited, nothing more.

"This is a nice place," she said, pressing her upturned face against my knee.

"Would you like to stay here?"

"In this room?"

"Here, or upstairs — anywhere you wish," I said softly.

"Your room is pretty."

"Did you enjoy it?"

"Yes." She smiled.

Harry approached. "I like it here," he announced. Ava looked at him and moved aside in disdain. I restrained my impulse to enter their quarrel. Harry's friendship, though tenuous, could be helpful.

"Do you wish to stay?" I asked him. At that moment, Edam bounded in, giving Harry no chance to reply. Glaring wildly, Edam pushed him so hard in the chest that he fell backwards to the floor. The rest tittered at Harry's position and drew close as if to watch a fight. Tom, Eenie, and Meenie descended from the sofa. Ava ran to Edam and tried to keep him from kicking Harry, who rose unsteadily to retaliate.

Although I would have relished Edam's defeat, Harry already seemed at a disadvantage. "No!" I protested. "Don't fight." I could have deftly picked up the antagonists, who would probably have shifted their fury to me. My voice momentarily shocked them. They resumed their grappling.

Ava cried for assistance. Isaiah, aided by Dick and

Tom, tried to pry the fighters apart. The scuffling and tug-
ging back and forth went on, but soon the three succeeded.

"Don't touch Ava! Don't ever touch her again!"
Edam shouted to Harry. If he had witnessed the chase
around the pole, had he also watched Ava rest her head
against my knee?

"Harry didn't hurt her," I blurted out.

"He did not hurt me," agreed Ava. "I saw him!" Edam
retorted. Then a general pronouncement, seemingly
directed at me, "He must not touch her again."

"It was only a game." Harry's tone was grim. Tom and
Dick relaxed their hold on his arms. Edam shook free of
Isaiah. "Play games with your own female," he warned.

Of all the creatures, Edam alone had a distaste for the
terms "woman" and "man" and had informed me that he
preferred "male" and "female" as references to his group.
It may have been a means of setting them apart from
humans, as if our nomenclature were distasteful and rep-
resented inferior beings. Edam's usage, moreover, seemed
to place him above his people, whom he consistently
referred to as "them" rather than "us" or "we," as if he
had escaped classification. Since it was still awkward for
me to accept the little beings as men and women, my own
attitude of superiority subtly corresponded to his. Edam's
rampant sexism, however, did bother me, not only as
adjunct to his authoritarian manner, but more pertinently
as it affected Ava.

Edam announced that it was time to leave; I gave up
hope of prolonging the stay. His bullying commands sub-
dued the grumbling that greeted his words. One by one
his comrades maneuvered the stairs after him.

Harry was the last to start. I met him halfway to the top. When he reached my step, he looked at me oddly, and I saw that his rage had not abated. "He will be sorry, that one," he muttered. "Wait and see."

"You and I are friends," I said. "Remember that." I tapped his shoulder for emphasis.

At the back door, everyone took leave of me gravely. Suddenly I felt that the visit had been a failure. I blamed no one, not even the detested Edam, more bitterly than myself.

VI
Purchase

The next morning I was awakened by distant thunder and glints of lightning. Through the grayness, I could see the thickening rain whipped across the lawn by the wind. My first thought was of the garden. The two shelters were secure. The large one was nailed to a shingle; the hutch had survived many assaults of weather. Nevertheless, I slipped into my thong sandals, put on my hooded slicker, and went out.

The creatures were standing near their houses by the foundation. They would venture beyond the drip line carved by the gutters until a shaft of wind sent them staggering back. "Come into my house," I offered immediately. "You will be safe there."

Ava and Harry advanced toward me. Edam stopped them, saying loudly, "Wait! We are safe here." Then he addressed me. "Thank you." It was more dismissal than courtesy. How I longed to speak my mind.

They continued discussing my invitation until the air suddenly blanched and thunder shook the ground, ending the talk. Ava and Edam entered the hutch; the others disappeared next door. Rain came down like retribution, loosening the earth into mud under my sandals as I walked back to the house.

All morning and afternoon I stayed indoors, watching the storm surge in waves while I wandered from room to room. I made tea and was rattled by the whistle of the kettle. The lights dimmed but the electricity did not go off; a neighbor from the old days of my existence called, supposedly to see if I were all right and actually just feeling lonely himself. I was uncommunicative, perhaps to the point of rudeness, and knew (with satisfaction, since I really wanted no prying eyes around me, certainly not now) that I would not hear from him again.

Once more thunder quivered the house, and I suddenly quailed at the thought of dying unnoticed, unmourned. If I called California, what would I say? Where were the words, the words unspoken? Fled, discarded somewhere in the garbage dump, carried away by seagulls and steamshovels. Since my new friends appeared, I was not interested in newspapers. My son! If only I could cry out once, join the thunder that was devastating the ordered silence of my days, toppling it like blocks. I wanted to call California and ask, "Did you love me then? Was I unlovable? Will you be a better father? Do you plan to have children? What is the weather like? Are you bored, knowing it will never snow, that the frost will not touch you? Do you think it will always be a golden summer?" We had exchanged some frosty words when he called months ago, after receiving his birthday check. Like me he felt injured; each of us thought the other should call. Our meager correspondence halted. I wondered whether he might call at Thanksgiving.

What were seasons to me, anyway? Raking leaves or mowing the lawn, wearing a sweater or no sweater, boots or no boots, pacing my land on Shoreview Road — where I was stranded! — or walking around the wooded block. I hardly ever descended to the bay or drove to the ocean, the stormy ocean I had loved to stare at as I sat alone in my car. What were holidays to me? Christmas? Scrooge was lucky. He had the Three Spirits. They showed him his place in the real world, while I was making a place in fantasy.

Suppose the garden people never returned to the house? They might go away. That would be the end of everything. I would be alone again. Yet I knew some of them would choose my house. I knew that. How to entice them there, and to stay? Even if they all did not, some would defy Edam and remain. They must.

And so the notion of clothing the group recurred to me seriously as a practical measure. I recalled my image of Ava, wigged and gowned, as she might appear before me. I remembered the pleasure with which everyone had handled my garments. Expecting Edam's resistance, I decided to conceal my intentions.

At noon, my stomach filling with a rumbling anxiety, I disciplined myself to eat a piece of toast with jam and a cup of hot tea. Food, no matter how meager, meant order, matters not getting out of hand. I donned my raincoat and sneakers, wrenched my umbrella off a closet hook, and hurried to the car. A pool of water was beginning to collect over the bluestones in the driveway.

At times rain flooded the windshield and I had to stop. Twenty miles ahead lay a large, neighboring town where I was unknown. The delays and the weather discouraged my resolve. I slowed down, ready to make a U-turn on the highway and retreat from an irrational path. Awake or asleep, was it not a nightmare just the same, a nightmare in which a man of my years and propriety was embarked upon buying doll clothes for improbable people? And could I hope to keep them to myself indefinitely? Did I have the right?

Their disclosure to the world could bring me wealth and fame. To what avail? I was not greedy; I had enough money to suit my needs. Fame seemed undesirable: my morsel of quiet existence would be chewed and spat out into the world. What a congregation of newspapermen, television cameras, impassioned attorneys quoting relentlessly, punctuated by picketers with banners proclaiming: A PERSON'S A PERSON NO MATTER HOW SMALL! Then the cheers, the weeping and shouts of approval as the verdict is announced. Legal theft!

I did have a right. The little ones were my life, and I was theirs. I could change my mind later on, but the choice was mine. My spirits lifted. I reached the town and parked the car in front of a large toy store. I opened my umbrella, walked rapidly out of the rain into the shop. The place was nearly empty.

A saleswoman charged at me. "I would like some doll clothes," I told her.

"For how tall a doll?"

"Twelve inches, more or less."

"You have to be exact," she confided. "And what kind of doll is it?"

I was taken aback. "I don't know."

"It's very important to know the kind. There are so many these days. Have you any idea? Is it a baby doll? Teenage? Chubby? Slim?"

"Oh, quite slim," I remarked hastily. "Adult-looking."

She beamed. "Ah, teenage. Like Barbie. They're so popular. I have just what you want." She led me to the counter.

"For a lucky little girl," she purred, indicating the display.

"Girls and boys," I clarified, distracted by the variety of articles. Her eyes widened.

"Girls' and boys' clothing," I added quickly. "There's a boy doll, too. Actually, there are several, male and female."

She looked at me, puzzled by my speech or manner, or both. I was intimidated.

"I have several grandchildren."

She buttered her expression with a smile. "Of course!" she gushed, approving.

"Five, in fact." I was being clever.

"Really? How marvelous."

"Each has a pair of dolls."

"What an indulgent grandpa!"

I crawled behind my smirk.

"We have Barbie and Ken-type articles—copies, but as good as the originals and much less expensive." She bustled about the sizable sale on a slow day.

Avoiding further conversation, I hurriedly made my selections and paid the bill. One could have outfitted ten people for the money—at least from a thrift shop.

Outside it was still raining. Discreetly, I placed my bag of purchases in the trunk of the car and drove off. I felt depressed. Something unpleasant had attached itself to me and I could not shake it off. I traveled faster, and it clung more tightly: my own image. Warped. Myself in a distorting mirror, myself in the toy shop on a fool's errand. Why had I gone there? Doll clothes were for dolls, the stuff of childhood. I was grotesque.

Yet was it my crime there were no grandchildren? And even if grandchildren existed, would they be meaningful in my life, or beyond embrace, like my son?

The garden had risen into my arid life as a spring. It was accessible to my touch as love must be touched, given and taken into the body, a communion. I was being nurtured, increased. I had become more than an aging, solitary man who received no letters.

Skidding around a curve alerted me to my speed and I slowed down. The rain diminished to a soft drizzle. In the driveway, I felt an impulse to rush to the garden with my invitation. Instead, I waited. By tomorrow, I hoped, time would prod both their curiosity and their will to leave the sodden ground.

VII
Sin

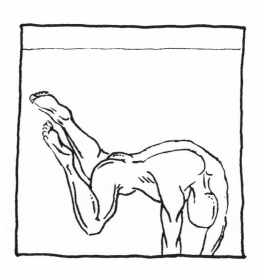

It was a brilliant morning. A few high clouds were drawn like wisps of veil across the sky; grass and leaves charged the landscape with color. My confusion had passed with the rain. I washed and dressed quickly. In the kitchen, I poured myself some orange juice. I could have skipped coffee, but chose instead to prolong my anticipation. After breakfast, I walked to the garden.

"Good morning!" I called cheerfully. Everyone seemed pleased to see me, except Edam. Ava came to stand near me.

"How were your shelters? Did the rain bother you?" The ground was damp, but the sun was evaporating all evidence of the storm.

"The shelters are good," said Edam. "We have been working," he added mysteriously.

"Look there!" Isaiah exclaimed, pointing to a small pile of odd-looking weeds. "They were coming up in the soil. We took them out this morning. The rain fed their roots too much." They had weeded the garden! It looked even barer than before.

"Thank you," I said dubiously. "You did well," I added, acknowledging their pride. The weeds were a pallid green and weirdly twisted. What would they have become? The ground people had acted in a proprietary way, brooking no further intrusions on their turf. They would not share the soil with newcomers.

No matter. Whatever else might flourish in that earth was of no consequence to me. The creatures could make their ground as bare as they wished. Only their presence was essential.

"I have something for you all," I said. "Presents. In the house."

"Your house?" Edam asked slyly.

"My house."

"Please, Edam," said Ava. "Let us go." The others watched him patiently for a sign. Harry, who stood apart, approached me. "I will come," he asserted.

"Thank you, Harry," snarled Edam. "We will go with you." I led the procession to the back door.

In the kitchen, my guests flocked around me. They followed me into the living room, neutral territory where I had spread the doll clothes upon the brown hooked rug. Soon the little feet were treading gingerly among tiny dresses, trousers, shirts, shoes, underwear. If the experiment worked, later on I would buy winter clothing.

"These are for everybody," I said. "Try them on." I sat on the floor and held up one of the dresses. It was a blue print with a pink sash. In the toy store, its fabric had recalled the texture of my rayon pajamas which the females had found so pleasing. "Oh!" sighed Ava. "That is so pretty!"

I handed her the dress and a pair of stocking tights, and saw that the shoes were too small, and had impossibly high heels. I pulled the collar over Ava's head while Mona tugged down the hem. The females crowded her admiringly, exclaiming, "Oh!" "Nice!" "Pretty!" Under Edam's stony gaze, I hesitated to assist Ava with her stockings and restricted myself to verbal directions. Eenie, Meenie, Minie, and Mona copied Ava's procedure, pressing their efforts with grunting and chatter. The males were keener to observe them than to take their own initiative. They seemed fascinated, as I was.

The little creatures were laying upon themselves the form and fabric of my world. The power of their strangeness was being mitigated by cloth, snaps and buttons that encased them like totems of my strength. Now they were small people and vulnerable.

Mona held up a pair of trousers she had tried to pull on, and induced Isaiah, glum and reluctant, to wear them. When the females were dressed, they badgered their companions to do likewise and eagerly assisted them. The reticence of the males seemed to make them awkward. I helped with a shirt snap here and there, or a twisted waistband. I encouraged the proceedings with a discourse on the virtues and development of clothing. I mentioned the evolution from nudity, omitting reference to early covering of the genital area which did not apply here, might perplex the group, and embarrass me. I emphasized the aesthetic value of colors and fabrics, and suggested as delicately as I could a relation between vesture and civilization. Due to nervousness, my speech was delivered nonstop. It came abruptly to an end when I saw that all were dressed.

As they walked about uncertainly, I feared they might be uncomfortable and precipitously disrobe. I thought of the dolls I had seen in a Christmas window display, moving stiffly across a changeless tableau. But these were self-willed dolls, beyond control, dolls only in size. The trepidation of the females dwindled as they admired each other. Among the males, opinion was divided. Harry stood inquiringly before Ava until she expressed her approval. When he walked away, Edam sullenly permitted her to adjust his shirt; Tom submitted to the ministrations of Eenie and Meenie. I took the mirror from the chest in my room and put it on the rug, hoping to reinforce their interest.

Everyone gathered at the mirror; it rewarded them with pleasing images. Only Isaiah showed distaste. He sat apart, enduring the whining entreaties of Mona, then started to remove his shirt. Fearing his attitude might be contagious, I tried coaxing. "Your shirt is made just like mine," I remarked inanely.

"It is so," he conceded. "But I have no need." I realized at once the glaring omission in my talk. "It will help keep you warm," I persisted.

"The weather is warm," Isaiah intoned morosely, and proceeded to remove his trousers.

"You will be more comfortable!" I went on, my voice rising. "Trousers will protect you when you sit upon the ground. It is more comfortable to sit on a blanket than on the bare earth. Yes," I continued rapidly, "clothes are like blankets, cushions—they cushion your body in every position, lying on your back, stomach, side, sitting down—and think of your elbows—" I broke off lamely.

"The earth is good to sit upon," droned Isaiah, his voice seeming to issue from a sepulcher. His pronouncement strongly affected Mona, who turned acquiescent. "The earth is good to sit upon," she echoed dispiritedly and began to disrobe.

As I watched her with dismay, Edam, who had taken Isaiah aside, spoke to him seriously. The rest, entranced, preened themselves at the mirror. My heart sank as Edam unfastened his shirt buttons and removed his clothes, announcing, "We have no need of these things. Let us go."

The protests surprised him. "No!" said Eenie, Meenie, and Harry. "Not yet!" said Tom and Dick and Minie. "Why?" despaired Ava.

"You did not hear Isaiah," Edam rebuked. "He said, 'The earth is good to sit upon.' That is true. Perhaps we can use it as our motto, like," and he pointed to the sampler on the wall, "'God Bless Our Home.' Is that not so, Joseph?"

He was mocking me, and I could do nothing but repress my fierce urge to hit him, one hard blow, or better, to trample him, squash him, stomp his hypocritical, arrogant cigar butt of a body into the rug. I thought of a blowfish out of water, puffing and puffing up. If only, like a blowfish, he would die.

"You will do as you wish," I replied stoically. How peculiar the word "God" on his lips! What right had he to utter a strictly human concept, corrupting it with a sneer? "The earth is good to sit upon": an expedient slogan he could use again, like the cudgel of a religion to thwart me. The cynic!

Ava stood disconsolately facing Edam. "Why?" she repeated. "I am happy with the clothes."

"Hurry up!" he snapped. "Do you wish us all to wait for you?"

Her head was bowed pitifully; I could barely keep from picking her up. "Come back any time," I announced. "Any of you. I shall save the clothes for you here. You are always welcome. Any time."

The others brightened at my words.

"We will come back when we decide to," said Edam. I mentally exchanged the second "we" for "I." There was no doubt that Edam would make the decision.

A sighing passed among the creatures. Isaiah and Mona assisted with the undressing, devoutly engaged in their task like perverse missionaries. Nudity was now sanctioned as righteousness. Clothing was evil. Judging by the wistful glances and murmurs, the ethic was unpopular. Ava fingered a miniature strand of pearls.

"You may keep it," I told her.

"Thank you!"

Edam scowled. "You will leave that here." She shot him a furious look that faded into resignation. "I will come back for it," she promised. I showed my guests to the door and held it open as they filed out past me. Several paused to thank me mournfully for my trouble.

"I hope we can come back," said Minie.

"We know you are our friend," said Harry.

"Do not think badly of us!" Ava called back. I waved,

smiling to conceal my pain, the pain that cried, Please don't leave me alone. Then I closed the door. That was the end of it. I became aware of water dripping into the kitchen sink and tightened both faucet handles, gripping them hard until my fingers ached. Silence fell about me like dust. I wanted to cry.

VIII
Exiles

I lay in bed, weighted and immobilized by gloom. Arising activity, life itself seemed purposeless. I thought of Oblomov in the Russian novel, lying in bed in his dressing-gown, pondering day after day whether to get up, listening to time in his own heartbeat. My mental picture was so alarming I forced myself to leave the bed and open the blinds. Although my side window gave an adequate view of the garden, I had avoided standing there, lest I be caught spying. But how could matters worsen? Edam had trapped me. His control now extended into my house.

I had planned to record my experiences; to date, I had not even begun. Removed bit by bit into a monstrous kind of daydream, I would disappear entirely. Paper could save me. In a way I was a creature of paper, of the paper mill I had gone to, fled to as a young man. Paper was true, it could assert life, it could be life. I opened the drawer of my night table, took up the empty notebook and pencil I had placed there so long ago, a notebook whose covers indicated a beginning and an end to stories in between. Secretly, I had always enjoyed books and writing. As a child, I had looked upon books as quiet friends. Authors who were there for me whenever I wished. But times were hard and my parents discouraged my literary interests. After my brother died, it was as if I had died, too. They directed me toward earning a living at a regular job, making certain that I could leave their unwelcoming house. Thrust into the business world as soon as I could get there, I seized what I mistook for independence and thrived in the marketplace, finally becoming its instrument. When I met Emma, I expected again to make a new life. But it was all a continuity; there was no change, because I was the same and had made the same choices. I cannot blame Emma; she had never tried to fool me. The terrible irony is that we matched.

I ran my fingers over the metal spiral that made an open spine of concentric circles. Could words, the making of logical sentences and entry of facts: could these fasten my reason? Prove that I was sane, still in charge of all aspects of me? Someone inside me laughed and would not be deceived. Madness did not always roll its eyes, flinging up fantastic visions. It could erect its house with an ordinary facade. Later would come the crumbling of an eccentric foundation.

Ah, but the ground people were real. My affection and anger were real. What was irrational was denying my senses because they revealed something extraordinary, unique. Madness lay elsewhere—perhaps in the

simple fact of my total isolation. And if the crazy compet-
itive world were to blame for spawning such contentious
creatures, for irradiating the earth with callousness,
greed, and stupidity, had I not participated in that world?
Didn't my detachment perpetuate it? Weren't the ground
people like me?

And with whom could I discuss them? —not even the
mailman. Not a single, caring person was available to me.
What a weird topic they would present in a letter to my
son! I hardly knew him well enough to be certain he
would understand or even be interested. He might think
I was crazy. Maybe he would like me better that way—
what a dour parent I must have seemed to him! A
monument in an armchair, reading the paper after dinner.
I ceased trying to imagine his reaction.

But I could speak to my journal. A therapeutic exer-
cise in communication. I admitted the need: Though the
words would reach only myself, they would connect with
something outside me, something dependable, making no
demands.

I went to the window and looked out. Most of the
garden was visible. The area adjacent to the house could
not be seen unless I opened the window and protruded
my head. I drew up a chair and sat, writing.

Tuesday, mid-August

*A sunny day. Harry passes Edam and they both
turn away. I don't think they exchanged a word. Isaiah
and Mona walk into the woods. I cannot see Ava. Is she
in her house?*

Very little "bird language" is used anymore. Is their use of English an accommodation to me, an affectation, or a natural process, that is to say, a maturation?

Minie sits idly tossing pebbles at a stone. I cannot see Dick. Eenie and Meenie are directly below me. Tom stands with them, shaking his head. Eenie mentions my name and the word "clothes" is repeated clearly, with Tom shaking his head vigorously. Meenie babbles. I make out the sentence, "We want to wear them." Tom says something about Edam and Isaiah and "female silly ways" upon which they begin to push him. He pushes back. They scream and he scrambles toward Minie, who continues playing with the pebbles. He sits beside her. She gets up, he grabs her hand, and she pulls back. Another game? Tom wrestles her to the ground. She kicks and shouts . . .

I dropped my pencil and notebook and ran outside. When I reached the garden, I found Eenie and Meenie staring nonchalantly at the struggle. They were angry with Tom and disliked Minie. Edam stood near his house with arms folded, smiling. Ava hurried to the grappling pair. Dick overtook her. Grasping Tom by the shoulders, he pulled him off Minie so violently that he fell.

"Stay away from her!" Dick raged.

"I don't take orders from you! Only Edam gives orders. Go away." Tom rose unsteadily.

"I said stay away from her!" Dick emphasized with a push that sent Tom stumbling. Tom crouched, then ran straight at Dick's middle. His target hopped aside and Tom went sprawling. Dick jumped on his back and they rolled over, pummeling each other's head, Tom pushing up Dick's chin and trying vainly to gouge out an eye. There was no bleeding, no bruises appeared, but the grimaces and moans attested to severe pain mutually inflicted.

Watching, I felt excitement, but quickly responded to my twinge of conscience by calling out "Stop it!" They went on fighting.

Edam moved closer, eyes shining. "Why don't you stop them?" I told him irritably.

"It is their business," he replied. "Is that not the expression?"

"The expression is correct, not the attitude," I retorted.

"Aha!" Edam laughed. "You remain the teacher. But we are no longer your pupils."

Tom was being beaten. Harry stood by and Ava moaned, "No ! No !", her protests joined by Eenie and Meenie.

Edam called out sharply, "Stop it! Enough."

Dick seemed deaf and blind to all save Tom's head, which he pounded from side to side with an implacable rhythm. "Stop it!" Edam repeated. "I order you."

When Dick continued, Edam advanced and slapped his face, shouting, "How dare you disobey me!"

Eenie and Meenie rushed to Tom, who lay motionless on the ground. Though his head looked weird, out of shape, dented and flattened in spots, no discoloration was evident. Eenie cradled Tom's battered head and wailed. Meenie knelt beside him, punctuating murmurs of sympathy with insults cast at Dick, who now stood abjectly a few steps back with the onlookers. "Killer! Beast!" she shouted.

Edam grabbed him roughly and said, "This is the end for you."

"What do you mean?"

"You will get out. Right now."

Incredulous, Dick asked, "Where shall I go?"

"That is your business."

"I can't believe—that you intend—" He broke off. "I did not know Tom was important to you."

Edam laughed. "He is of no special importance. I cannot tolerate what you did."

"What was that?"

"You disobeyed me. That is a crime here."

"I don't believe it. I don't accept it."

"The more reason for you to go."

"Unfair! Unfair!" Minie rushed to Dick and took his hand. "He was trying to protect me! I should be the one to leave."

Edam shifted his wrath. "Do not tell me what is fair. You will be sorry."

"I will go with him!" sobbed Minie. "I don't want to stay here." She threw her arms around Dick and began to cry tearlessly. He patted her shoulder.

"The woods are full of wild animals," he said. "It is hard to live there."

I was touched. "You are welcome to stay with me." Everyone looked up.

Edam seemed disconcerted. "Why do you concern yourself?"

"There is room in my house for many, and you are my friends."

"We feel toward you as you toward us." He was laughing at me. "You trouble yourself too much for us. We are such little people."

His sarcasm was infuriating. "No trouble at all. I esteem your friendship."

"Certainly."

Minie held Dick's hand. "We will stay with you," she asserted. "Thank you."

"Do not ever come back!" Edam warned.

"We will not want to," said Dick.

"Get out of here! Go away—both of you!" Edam screamed in a tantrum. "You will be sorry!"

The couple left the garden. Edam strode to his house and slammed the door. Tom recovered enough to sit up and enjoy the fussing over him by Eenie and Meenie, and Isaiah and Mona who had just returned.

Ava stood apart. "I hope Minie and Dick will be happy," she told me.

"So do I. Perhaps you can visit them. And me. The clothes will be here for you."

"Perhaps." Her tone was hopeless.

"Joseph!" Harry addressed me and beckoned me down to whisper. "Some day we will come, too." He gave Ava a meaningful stare and walked away. I trailed Dick and Minie over the flagstones.

IX

Dissent

S incere as my invitation had been, it was a strain that first evening, to have strangers around. How patiently they sat before the sofa, waiting. Told they had the freedom of the house, they trudged about for awhile, then resumed their vigil.

At dinnertime I asked the couple to join me at table. I set them upon the plastic cloth so they would be nearer my eye level. Requiring nothing themselves, watching me eat apparently distressed them. Conversation failed; halfway through the meal they asked to be excused. I put them back on the floor. They returned to the living room where the doll clothes were piled in an open box on the floor. They sat by the sofa, mournfully contemplating the rejected finery.

I finished my meal and left the kitchen feeling exhausted. Although I wanted to escape to my room, I was determined to be gracious. "Dick, if you and Minie would be more comfortable, you could have one of the bedrooms," I offered. "No, thank you," he replied.

I was surprised, since a bed seemed preferable to the hard sofa downstairs, and the creatures (at first) had delighted in my bed. "The air is good in the cellar," he explained.

"You mean the dampness?"

"It is like the night outside." Whether he was being honest or timid, I accepted the arrangement with relief. My privacy was salvaged.

I disguised my faulty hospitality with attention. Dick protested mildly, but I insisted on a bedsheet for the rattan sofa where he and Minie would sleep. I took a pillow and an acrilan blanket for good measure and ceremoniously led my guests down the steps. I imagined the dismay of a human-sized visitor confronting such accommodations.

While Dick and Minie debated the need for a blanket, I opened the sheet, bolstered the pillow against a sofa arm, and left the folded blanket at the opposite end. I attached long strings to two of the ceiling fixtures so that they could turn on lights; the other lights were controlled by the switch at the head of the stairs.

We took leave of each other politely and I ascended, leaving the cellar door secured ajar with a doorstop. The stove light faintly illumined the kitchen. I went through the house, switching off lights and checking locks. I locked my own door as well and collapsed fully clothed on my bed into a profound sleep.

The next morning I felt more miserable than ever. It was almost nine o'clock; my prolonged slumber had made me groggy. Painfully, I arose. From the bureau mirror an old, lined face gaped at me through swollen lids. Youthful residue: a shock of thinning hair, practically white. A nondescript face. Worry lines in a brow raised high over a thin nose; parentheses lines framing lips useless except for consuming things. Time had struck its messages, yet I could not decipher them all, and some were surely a joke, a cosmic joke.

How would my son behold this face? Bracketed in the garbage dump category of Old Man? Or would he see his father, generously remembered in some aspect of youth, smiling, a man who had bought a car and once taken his family on vacation out west for two weeks and sent his son to the best business school?

Behind my mirrored eyes, those tired old eyes, someone was crying. Had I learned nothing, accumulating age and experience like separate stones of a cairn? Perhaps I already lay entombed alive, naked and diminutive as the people from the ground.

I raised a slat of the blind. Ava sat alone at the edge of the garden. She glanced at my window as if she knew I was there. Her listless pose, her aloneness spoke to me. She rose obediently as Edam called. He was intolerable. I turned angrily from the window, unlocked my door, and left the room.

Dick and Minie were downstairs; I could not tell whether they were awake. Scanning the darkness, I could see them lying on the sofa under the sheet. My clanging about the kitchen making coffee soon brought them to me. They looked neither sleepy nor refreshed.

"Would you care to go outside?" I asked hopefully.

"No!" they replied.

They did not sit with me; I anticipated a serene breakfast. Finding a picture magazine in the living room, I set it down for them on the rug and returned to my coffee and toast.

How ironic that after desiring so strongly the companionship of the garden folk, I should prefer my usual solitary meal. I sympathized with the outcasts, who were beginning to register their exile from the group. In truth, however, my guests were tiresome; their presence had begun to oppress me. They were a couple (odd, indeed), moreover, and I was single. Sometimes I would look at them and feel that I was the grotesque, the displaced. Why had I been impetuous? My generous impulse did strengthen my position with a few members of the group. I had wanted to thwart Edam, showing the others, especially Ava, my superior qualities and resources. My guests were a connection with her, perhaps even a sort of bait. But my unhappiness with Minie and Dick punished my pride, converting the hubris of Greek tragedy into farce. One fact propelled me toward some nebulous action, like a shadow crouching in a corner of myself. Yes, I wanted Ava in my house and no one else. The remaining coffee grew tepid in my cup.

Dick and Minie were enjoying the magazine. They held it open on the floor and kneeled at the bottom of the pages. Pictures and colors fascinated them. I proposed teaching them to read; they accepted gladly. There would be something interesting for us to do.

Remembering an old alphabet book of my son's in the bookcase, I found several primers as well. Emma had kept them. She had also saved his infant's clothing and his copybooks, put them into drawers among her own things, as if these gave tangible evidence of her possession. After a long day's work, when I sat reading my newspaper after dinner, she would send him to me with whatever questions he might have about school. I suppose I was uncharitable, thinking she deliberately had him pester me when I was resting. Yes, that was unfair, but I was weary of her obvious preference that opposed us into rival siblings. Late one afternoon, when our adolescent son was out playing ball with friends, I remember her sitting on our bed, caressing a woolen bunting as if it still held a baby, and replacing it reverently into the large box of tiny clothes.

"Things cannot save the past for you," I told her maliciously. "There is only the treasury of the mind." Of course this contradicted the whole conduct of my life, its race to get ahead, so I was partly malicious and partly honest, revealing what must have been—or was unconsciously becoming for me—a deep truth. Before my recent adventure, I had always felt depleted by time, never enriched.

I showed the books to Dick and Minie who, with eager attention, learned the alphabet almost immediately. Yet after about fifteen minutes, they seemed restless. Short attention span—or fatigue induced by the unusual effort of concentration? They agreed, however, to resume the lesson the following day. Again I invited them outdoors and they declined. Probably they feared meeting Edam, the Wrath of Edam.

"You won't mind my going out for awhile, will you?" I asked rhetorically.

"No, Joseph, if you wish to go."

Ignoring Dick's dubious tone, I stepped out into the sunshine. The earth was green. Exhilarated, I walked through the patio to the garden where Harry was at work on a pile of twigs and branches. With a kind of fury, he sawed a branch in half. Ava sat near him on a stone. Looking doleful, she gave me a fleeting half-smile. Neither seemed inclined to speak. They were alone.

I drew up an aluminum chair and sat close by. "What is the matter?"

"Nothing." Harry grimly assaulted the wood.

"Where is everyone?" I persisted. Ava began pacing. Harry dropped the tip of the saw to the ground and leaned on the handle.

"They are up in the trees!" he snapped. "Edam will tell them they are birds, and then they will spread their arms and fly. Ha!" He was very angry.

"I am not to stop working," he went on, applying the saw once more. "Edam, or one of his spies, Isaiah or Tom, might see me. I don't mind a battle, but it is not what I want." He fell silent.

"I don't understand—why are they in the trees?"

Harry paused again. "Because Edam told them to go. Because Edam said we should move to the trees, build shelters there. We are going to have daily tree-climbings, so we can climb up fast, in case."

"In case what?"

"In case something terrible happens."

"Suppose it happens too quickly, what then?"

"Edam says we should not be on the ground anymore. Perhaps he does not want to be near you. He says that up in the trees we will be protected from everything."

"That's ridiculous! Squirrels can climb trees. And there is always a force that can destroy what you build. You control what you can. Does Edam rule the air? The wind moves everything. A strong wind—we even have hurricanes, the strongest of winds—and the shelters will come crashing down."

"He said that on the ground we will face the burrowing animals. He may be right. I think our old shelters are good enough. The others are too frightened to oppose him. Well, I do not care."

I turned to Ava. "Why did you not go with them?"

"I opposed Edam. In front of everyone." Her voice was flat and weary. "I told him the tree shelters were foolishness. I said we would be safer in your cellar. He hit me. He said I did not deserve to look for the sites. I replied that I had no wish to go. He forbade me, to make my staying a punishment. I wish I were far away from here!"

She dropped to her knees, uttering tearless, gurgling sobs. She flung her arms about my knee, and I stroked them gently with my fingertips. How cool they felt in the summer's heat! Perspiration coursed down my armpits and pasted my shirt to my back.

Harry helped her to rise. He held Ava's hand as he addressed me. "I am punished also. Not by work—work is a game to me. No, my punishment is to guard Ava. That is Edam's way." He dropped her hand.

"Edam should not make us suffer," Ava said simply. Harry stared at the trees behind the lawn. "They are coming back." Then he whispered to me, "Leave your door open tonight. The kitchen one. I must speak to you and Dick. Go now, if you do not want to see Edam."

At this point I certainly had no wish to see him. I hardly dared to have him within my grasp! Avoiding a backward glance, I rose and walked straight ahead to the front lawn, past the azaleas and taxus beneath the windows, and entered the house. "Dick! Minie!" I called into the living room. "Tonight we shall have a visitor."

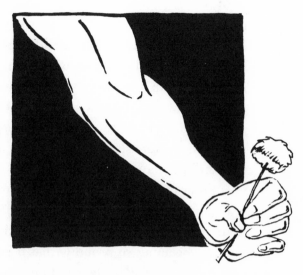

X

Beyond Evil

After clearing away the dinner dishes, I resumed my seat at the table, facing the back door. I found my mark in Thoreau's Walden, which I had begun to reread earlier in the summer. Dick and Minie came into the kitchen; this time I was pleased to have their company. They sat on the floor, observing the night through the screen door.

It was difficult to concentrate. After reading the same paragraph for the third time, I shut the book and got up to reheat some coffee.

A fragrant coolness flowed from outside, bringing in the sweetness of honeysuckle, and I remembered the baby snatching blossoms as my wife carried him. She looked beautiful at that moment in the road, gazing at his face. He was nearly two and had spoken early, probably thanks to her constant chatter. She had taught him the word "honeysuckle" and the taste of nectar that lay within the flower. He would say, "N-get honey suckoo, Mommy." He was an easy child, smiling, the kind who learned not to bother you (except for the missions inspired by his mother). We fished together a few times — now that comes back to me! — but we caught mostly blowfish, those dull weights on the line, so unlike the exciting bluefish who hit the lure and struggled to be free. I didn't have time, really, until I retired, and my son was gone by then. Did he understand, when he stood with his mother, facing me on graduation day as I took their picture — did he understand, with his earnest look and she beaming so proudly, that it could not have been otherwise, or that at least, though paltry, insufficient, lacking, all those unsatisfactory things, at least I had done my best?

And yet, if in the end life had awarded me its empty palm, I realized that I still retained something, a persistent weed of vitality, one that sprouted me here, waiting with my residue of hope focused upon the kitchen door.

"He may come soon," Dick uttered, breaking the silence. "After the sun disappears, everyone sleeps."

"I hope so." I poured myself some coffee and leaned back against the counter, opposite the door. Suppositions flew in and out of my mind, attaching themselves to moments like the moths and beetles flinging themselves at the screen, skittering away to return in greater numbers. I vacillated between confidence, that viewed the meeting as my taking charge of events, and doubt, that judged me as a prisoner of my weakness. Enthusiasm could be treacherous, so I clung to facts: the door, the night, insects, the proposed meeting. Emotion sought another path, however, filling me with an impulse to run away, the old impulse to avoid troublesome contacts. I should probably open the door, invite Dick and Minie to leave (I could literally kick them out as they sat on the floor, even sweep them out with my long-handled broom wedged beside the refrigerator), and have done with the whole business.

It was eleven o'clock. Dick shifted his legs restlessly, while Minie was gradually falling asleep. She lay with her head on his shoulder, her eyelids about to close. Whenever I thought she was dozing, she would open her eyes very wide in an effort to stay awake. I made a game of guessing how many more times she would open her eyes before shutting them in slumber, until I noticed that Dick had become rigid, his head straining forward as if listening for a particular sound. He moved Minie's head tenderly off his shoulder and she sat up, fully awake. He got up and went to the door. I stood immobilized.

"It is Harry!"

Crossing quickly to the door, I could make out a small figure and let him in. It was Harry, agitated. "Please close this too," he said, indicating the wooden door. I obliged.

We went to the living room and he had me check the doors and windows and draw the curtains and blinds. His nervousness was contagious. We sat on the rug, facing him, and he began.

"My situation is dangerous. I have taken the greatest risk. Tomorrow I may die." When we started to question him, he raised his hands. "Listen. You know what has become of us. You know what Edam has made of us. The ants and the worms have greater joy than we. Now the garden is an evil place. Edam has done this."

He paused, turning to Dick who nodded agreement, then continued. "Each one suffers, yet each one does nothing. He sent away Dick and Minie. They had a right to stay. He torments me because I do not yield. He makes Ava unhappy. And now he will put us all in the trees. He is hateful. He cannot use us any longer for his games."

"You could stay here," I said.

"That is impossible," Harry snapped. "Edam hates me. I will not hide in the house, afraid of how he might punish me. I will not leave without Ava. If I bring her here, he will find a way to kill me. And maybe everyone else in the house."

"That is true," said Dick. "He would not let you take her. He would not let you go. And he would blame us all."

This was it, the danger, the nebulous shape in the darkness.

"I wish Ava were here," sighed Minie. "I like to talk to her. It would be nice if you both lived here," she observed wistfully to Harry.

"Yes it would, but there is only one way that can be."

"One way?"

"We will have to kill Edam."

Minie blinked. Dick shook his head. Why did the thought seem familiar to me?

"There should be another way," said Dick, heavily.

Harry smiled. "Are you afraid of him?"

"Yes, I am afraid."

"Then I can do it."

Dick seemed puzzled. "What do you want of me?"

"Your help, afterwards. To bury him."

"And me?" I asked.

"To dig a deep hole in the sand. To shelter us, afterwards."

"There is sand at the foot of the driveway. And you are welcome here."

"With Ava?"

"Yes."

Minie sat with her hands clasped tightly. "We should not do this," she said softly. "We should not kill one of us."

Harry was irritated. "Leave Dick alone! He must choose to be a worm or a man."

I was amused to hear Dick referred to as a man. How puny a being! Yet who should decide how tall a real man had to be? Physical size was not the mark. It did not determine one's stature or status as a moral being. Harry was right. A man who acted like a worm deserved to be treated as one.

"Dick," said Harry, lowering his voice, "You must decide. This work is for you and me. Joseph would be discovered, because of his size. We are the ones to do this. Some day, everyone will thank you. Edam harms us all."

"I do not want to kill anything!" Dick protested.

"Leave the killing to me. I just need you to help me carry him."

"Ah."

"Do you hesitate?" Harry goaded. "Edam turned you out of your home. Were you happy he did that? Would you like to return, some day?"

"Oh, yes!" replied Dick. "I would like to return."

"As long as Edam lives, you can never go back."

Minie shook her head. "The others will hate us. They will not want us there. They might kill us."

"You are a fool!" sneered Harry. "They will forget. After awhile, they will welcome you."

Minie remained silent, her head bowed. "I don't know," murmured Dick. "Tell me," persisted Harry, "do you hate Edam?"

"Yes!"

"Has he not humbled you, stolen your home, your pride? Are you so fearful that you dare not help yourself?"

"Dick does not think only of himself," Minie put in.

"Then he must think of all of us. Of you."

"I am content," she insisted.

"I do not believe that! This is a bad life for you, to be in terror that Edam may seek to punish you again; to hide when you have a right to be outdoors. One day you will want to go out. What will you do?"

"I am not sure," said Minie faintly.

Harry was jubilant. "Of course you are not sure. You can never be sure. How do you know what Edam plans to do to you? He consults no one. Yet he expects to be obeyed. And he is."

Minie stared at the floor. Harry turned to Dick. "Do you agree with me?"

"Yes," he answered glumly, "I agree."

"You will help?"

"Yes."

"Then we must work quickly. Now."

"Tonight?" Dick was taken aback.

"Right away. I cannot go back. Edam will know or suspect—it is all the same. We have to do the job tonight."

The word "job" reverberated. Murder as work.

Dick became thoughtful again. "I see."

"How will you do it?" I asked Harry, trying to even my tone.

"We need something sharp."

"Like a nail?" I suggested, repelled by my helpfulness.

"No. A knife. A very small knife."

I remembered the children's tools I had bought. Nothing among them would do. I thought of the two penknives in my tackle box, retrieved and opened them. Harry found them clumsy. I got him an old straight razor from the bathroom, but it was difficult to hold. My kitchen knives were too large or too bulky.

He took up the smaller penknife again with both hands and said, "I will use this." He raised it over his head and brought it down with a snap of his arms. How efficiently he had sawed wood! "Yes," he reflected, "this will do it well." He smote the air.

"Oh!" shuddered Minie.

Harry glared at her. "Joseph," he said, "I wish you to do two things." I waited. "First, please do not let Minie see us with the body. She would be—upset."

"All right."

"Ava will come first. She should stay with Minie, away from the door."

"I will see to that."

"Second, you must help us now. We need a hole, a deep hole in the sand. You can dig faster that we, and it should be ready. There is little time."

"I will get my shovel."

I tiptoed down the cellar steps, leaving the door open to the discreet light from upstairs. The basement lights would make me visible from the garden. In addition to those in the shed, there were a number of tools downstairs. I found an ancient, heavy shovel and carried it upstairs. Harry was impressed with its size and wanted to supervise the digging. Minie, reluctant to be left alone, kept Dick with her, so Harry and I went out together, moving stealthily over the grass in the moonlight and then across the driveway to the sand. I glanced back, noting that the façade of the house had become somewhat unfamiliar, even sinister.

We stood at the mound. I lifted the shovel, bringing it down with ponderous stabs into the sand. God, I thought, I am digging a grave. I thought: the creature for this tomb came out of my ground. To that extent I was responsible for giving it life and would now preside over its death.

I felt a sudden rage that Harry was using me, thrusting me into the role of accomplice. As I retracted the shovel before the next jab into the deepening hole, I thought of swinging it behind Harry and toppling him into the pit, covering him with the sand before he could react.

It was unlikely that I could catch him by surprise. Besides, he was doing something indirectly for me that I could not do for myself. Thus moral qualms deferred to self-interest. The way of the world.

Harry waved his arms and whispered, "That is enough!" I put down the shovel and we returned to the house.

Seated in the living room, Dick sat with Minie, holding her hand. She was trembling, her mouth agape. "Go downstairs!" Harry ordered.

"Why?" from the couple.

"You bother me," to Minie.

"She does not want to be alone," Dick explained sheepishly. "Someone will have to stay with her."

"Joseph will stay. He will open the door for Ava, who will remain with Minie. Then Joseph will come outside to the hole and help us with his shovel."

I visualized the scene, repelled. "I might be needed inside." Now I was sounding like Dick.

"For what?"

"An emergency."

Harry would not be fooled. "No. You will help us."

Looking down at Harry, whose tone reminded me of Edam's brusque commands, I acquiesced.

Dick patted Minie's hands and whispered to her. He joined us at the door, where Harry was examining the penknife. I unhooked the screen door and they slipped out, Dick trailing behind.

I waited uneasily at the kitchen door, trying once more to void my mind, replenishing it with sense impressions free of conscience or remorse. Through the glass panes I followed every sallow illumination in the darkness where moonlight ranged ominously toward the woods. The lilac bushes huddled and the rose of sharon buds flinched from sight. A large yew by the driveway obscurely massed its branches.

A figure moved and I felt my blood pound and recede: it was Ava. I let her in and she fled past me without a word. Minie rushed to her and they embraced.

Back at my post in the darkened kitchen, leaning against the screen, my breath came in short spurts. I took a handkerchief from my pocket and mopped the trickle of perspiration creeping down my cheek. A faint sound: was it a pebble? A leaf? All at once they were coming around the corner of the house. They had done it.

Dick came first, the body slung prone over his shoulder; he was clutching the backs of the legs that hung stiffly like a forked twig. Close behind walked Harry, holding the penknife with both hands, a round object tucked under his arm. As Dick strained on along the driveway, Harry set down the object near the rhododendrons beside the house, and I could see it clearly. It was Edam's head.

Harry plunged the knife into the earth at the base of the bush and covered it with leaves. He glanced around, unaware of my presence. Automatically, I withdrew behind the doorjamb. A moment later he came up to the screen and tapped it with his fist. I stepped outside, accompanying him silently to the sand pit.

Hideous as the sight was, a hysterical laugh bubbled within me as I glimpsed Edam's head bulging out of Harry's armpit. So neatly plucked, without a sign of blood or animation, it seemed no more than a fruit detached from a stem.

How absurd to think of these creatures in human terms! Ridiculous to judge morally my behavior with them. They were nothing like me.

Dick heaved the body into the pit. I told myself that Edam, like the others, was a thing, his lifelessness merely underscoring the fact. Harry tossed in the head. I choked back a giggle and set to work, dropping shovelfuls of sand into the hole. The small body was covered quickly. Where were the mourners? This was no funeral, like the burial of my son's dead pets or my wife going into the ground. It was furtive, a criminal act.

My paper mask of detachment was falling away.

I vainly thought of Edam simply as matter, already beginning to decompose in the sand. I recalled my son's dead cat and rabbit, beings he had loved, now rotted in the earth near the garden; Emma's body in another stage of decay, moving inexorably toward that moment when casket and body sheathed in its taupe gown worn to our son's graduation would all crumble into each other.

Death lay at the bottom of the pit, the death of an insignificant creature, to be sure, but the layers of death I had heaped upon it suddenly stifled me and I turned away. Carrying my shovel before me, its weight pulled me groundward. I led the others single file in a deliberate procession that at last, I thought, had the style, if not the tone, of a funeral.

XI

Indoors

We entered a quiet house. Harry and Dick hugged the ladies. I took a bottle of Scotch from the cabinet beneath the counter, poured quite a lot into a glass, and drank it warm. Pausing by the kitchen table, I pressed down heavily with my palms, drawing in its solidity. I contemplated getting drunk, spewing my unpleasant thoughts, evicting the three personae non grata, and living happily ever after with Ava.

My uneasiness rose, fluctuating between dread and anger. Nothing would be the same again. Events grew irregular, jagged. From a nest of predictability, I had fallen toward a ground of novelty and danger, a package deal of love, murder, arrogance, servility, destruction, rebuilding, creation: life.

But what had I gained, except anxiety? In the living room sat two miniature couples, largely oblivious of me.

Hardly a satisfaction — to observe Harry pawing Ava.
A human being would show decorum.

Ava looked sad. Was she thinking about the deed —
her part in it? How could it have taken place without her
consent, if not participation? If she had left before the
act, she must have known what was impending. There
was time to warn Edam, or to awaken the others.

No. She was too delicate, too childlike to be conniv-
ing. At worst, Edam had brutalized her into passivity.
She had taken no part in his death. I yearned to brush
Harry aside like a fly.

Although no one discussed the act, it could not be dis-
missed. The shovelfuls of silence heaped upon it seemed
more to augment than to hide the deed.

"Ava is tired," said Harry. "She must sleep."

"She may stay wherever she likes," I offered. "She
would be comfortable here in one of the bedrooms."

"We can stay downstairs with Dick and Minie." The
plural pronoun was unpleasant but expected.

"You can both stay here." Upstairs, at least, Ava
would be closer to me. "What does she prefer?"

Harry seemed unsure of himself. In time he would
learn not to hesitate. Like Edam. He asked, "Ava, where
do you wish to stay?"

She stared at the wall. Shaking her head, she began,
"I do not care — " when she looked up at me. Her voice
became softer. "Here, in a room." Aware of my small vic-
tory, I hastened to close the subject and showed them the
guest bedroom, the small one farthest from mine. "You
will not be disturbed here."

Harry weighed the matter. "If you wish," he told Ava.

I pulled down the two blue bedspreads and placed the kitchen stepstool at the foot of one and a chair and stool beside the other, enabling them to climb more easily. I assumed both beds would be occupied.

Ava and Harry stood on the scatter rug between the twin beds. As I turned to go, Ava rushed toward me. She flung herself at my leg, clutching it tightly with her thin arms. Then she withdrew, composing herself. If she had been capable of tears, I would surely have seen them.

"Thank you," was all she said.

The sound of the closing door pained me, and I mused over Harry's difficulty in opening it again, his climbing on the stool and wrestling with the knob, or falling off. A new guilt overwhelmed me. Had I abandoned Ava, hid her wretchedness behind the door?

Dick and Minie were waiting at the cellar entrance. We bade each other goodnight, and they descended.

I felt exhausted. After checking the doors and the lights, averting my head I passed Harry and Ava's room and entered my own. I shut the door, making a listless survey of my bed, my furnishings, the forms and scope of my isolation. I fell upon the bed, hands clutching the air. At last I sank into a sleep troubled with cries and shadows and a dark, shapeless presence that whirled around me.

In the morning I was so tired that my sleep seemed like the fragment of a day's weary journey. I lingered in bed, savoring the minor aches distributed through my back and legs. Once on my feet, I stretched my arms upward, then extended them timorously downward toward my toes. At the garden window, I carefully raised one of the slats and peered through the blind.

No one stirred. If the creatures were hiding in their shelter, I could not see them. I decided to keep the windows and doors locked and the blinds closed until the situation was clarified.

In the kitchen, as I ate my breakfast the others joined me. I soon realized that we were to be a solemn group. The desultory conversation depressed me further, and Dick kept worrying aloud. "How long should we wait here? How will they receive us? What do they know? What do they think? What is happening?" Minie, withdrawn as ever, floated about him in a kind of suspension. Let them leave!

Ava distressed me. In her eyes I detected reproach, a faint, almost tender rebuke that fell upon me like the wings of a moth. Although she was cordial with Harry, from time to time she would drop out of their conversation into a morose silence which he seemed to ignore.

Harry obviously prized Ava regardless of her sentiments, whatever they might be. She was a trophy, the tangible evidence that he had won. Of us all, he was probably the most relaxed. His sated energies had temporarily come to rest.

Dick's monologue ran on. "Will they look for us? Can they attack us in the house? They must know about Edam. Are they angry? How angry? I wish we knew."

I tried to cheer him, to no avail. Eventually I gave up and avoided him. Even Harry found him irritating. "Enough!" he told him. "We have to wait here another day or two. We cannot return when anger is fresh. Is that clear?" Dick remained jittery.

Our confined idleness heightened the tension. I was too jumpy to read. No plumbing or carpentry or wiring

needed repair; I had learned to do these things in defense
of my privacy. I could teach a game: checkers, chess,
cards. Miniature sets were available. But I didn't like
cards much, and the other games would occupy us in
pairs, with me the likely candidate for eventual exclusion.
Recalling the ease with which Dick and Minie had begun
to read, I decided to teach the group.

Teacher, father, God. A big cheese — the biggest
Edam, also home-grown! I had the power of knowledge,
a swath of omniscience which I could bestow and share.
But it wasn't like teaching a child. I remembered helping
my son with arithmetic once or twice; I had been good
with numbers. Had I shown my impatience? Though I
didn't tell him I was disappointed, or don't recall telling
him, he stopped bothering me for assistance. For all their
quickness, however, Dick and Minie had been less satis-
fying. I wondered about this. When I suggested resuming
the instruction, my first pupils were less than enthusias-
tic, a reflection on my pedagogy or their diligence, or
both. Harry looked to Ava. When she showed interest, he
agreed. Then Dick and Minie assented.

The class gathered before me on the floor, and I
reviewed the primers I had shown. Noting Ava's blissful
attention to the pictures and words, I knew that as eager
a student as she might be, it was my voice that held her.

Dick became restless, drawing Minie's concentration
away from the book toward himself. He stood up,
thanked me, and with Minie in tow, wandered preoccu-
pied throughout the house.

Initially, Harry seemed the best pupil. His immediate
comprehension amazed me even more than that of his

peers. He soon tired, however, and lay back, contemplating the ceiling.

Ava's attention never lagged. Her intensity was visible in the way she strained forward, repeating the words in triumph as she promptly learned them. She gazed at me with a delight I hoped was personal. A glimmer of my sentiments may have stirred her, for she studied the book less and less until her eyes were fixed upon me. In the end, it was I who terminated the lesson and walked to the picture window.

A few oak leaves were falling on the lawn. So soon. . . the mass dying would begin, and I would start the raking, the tidying, the burning. One day I would look up at bereaved branches and a cold sky. I would be alone again, have the scene to myself again. How bitter that solitude would be! Dick and Minie gone. No matter. Harry—taking Ava with him as I knew he intended to— what would be left for me? Pain in exchange for peace. Harry neither deserved her nor made her happy. I could not permit life to be so unfair.

The garden people might reject Harry and Ava; there was that possibility. But what was the use of having things as they were—the visit prolonged indefinitely? Unbearably! The constant sight of Ava with Harry would be the worst misfortune of all.

Somehow the day passed. We retired early; it was a way to evade one another. I ran the water for a hot bath to relax my nerves. In the tub I lay back and closed my eyes. I pictured Harry and Ava in the room next door. The soap fell into the water, and sank. It was a pale soap, the color of Harry's skin, a round soap lying at the bottom like a drowned head.

My hands: patterned with veins in high relief, the hands of an old man. I thought of them holding Ava's tiny, smooth body, clutching at youth, at life itself. I soaped the washcloth and drew up my knee to scrub my leg. My limbs were not old; part of me reflected a past vigor. The face did not matter too much. It had existed.

I emerged from the tub feeling stimulated rather than eased. I put on fresh pajamas and went to my room, remarking that Harry had closed his door. I closed mine. In bed, thinking of that door and those behind it, sleep would not come.

What is going on? I wondered. What is he doing to her? In the human sense, he could do nothing—as far as I had observed—outside the most superficial contact. Yet I hated his even touching her. And what was her response, there in the darkness?

If Harry were repugnant to Ava, I thought, she would escape him, return to the garden. Were passivity, guilt, enough to bind her to him? Or was there another reason? Did she stay to be near me? I grew impatient with guesses. I needed to be sure of her regard. How could I, since Harry never left us alone? By design or accident, in my presence he was always by her side.

The next day I avoided Harry as much as possible. Hostility was gradually settling in my expression; it became difficult to remove the evidence at will. I had to leave the house, whatever the risk. Informing my guests that I needed a few groceries from the village, I assured them that the doors would be locked securely during my absence. Harry had insisted that another day should pass before anyone left the house or re-entered the garden.

I was bypassing his opinion, rationalizing that I had nothing to fear from the ground people. Harry, not I, was responsible for Edam's death.

I backed out of the driveway and zoomed down the road. I wanted to see water—not the willful, unpredictable ocean, but the bay, to reach its calm into me and ease my turbulence. At the end of the road, however, at the edge of sand sloping gently to the water, I saw a car. I was afraid to see anyone, as if another person would automatically invade, search, and destroy. Suffused by anger and frustration, I realized that I was driving around in circles. I headed for the grocery store, made my purchases, and returned.

A chipmunk scurried across the bluestones of the driveway into an oak tree. Nothing else moved. At the back door I resisted a temptation to visit the garden.

My four guests sat in the living room, absorbed in animated discussion. They scarcely noticed me. I removed the milk, tuna fish, and bread from the bag and placed them in the refrigerator. After setting the canned spaghetti and meat balls and canned stew in the cupboard, I stood at the threshold of the living room.

Harry addressed me from the floor. "We are making plans."

"What have you decided?" I asked politely, joining them on the rug.

"We are going back to the garden."

His words fell like a judge's sentence.

"Not so!" cried Ava. "Dick and Minie go tomorrow. They will return and tell us whether we are wanted. Then—then we will see—"

"Tomorrow we shall leave," interrupted Harry.

"No!" Ava looked at me imploringly. "We can stay here! Is that not what you told us?"

"You are welcome always," I said softly.

"Night is cold in the garden. I am happy here."

Harry laughed. "Joseph has enticed you with his pretty clothes."

"I do not think of them!"

"You would like to dress up every day, have all the clothes to yourself," Harry taunted.

"You are unkind!" she protested. "Joseph—you do not believe that, do you?"

"Of course not. I don't imagine Harry does, either."

Harry glared at me, then turned to Ava. "Very well," he went on gruffly. "Dick and Minie will go first. If we are welcome in the garden, we will go, too." His firm tone could not spoil my satisfaction: Ava had wanted to stay.

Harry seemed to change toward me from that moment. His dislike was nearly visible, an aura radiating from him whenever I appeared. With no attempt to disguise his feelings, he avoided me; guarding his prize, he kept Ava closer. At times, catching a whiff of the odor that had felled me in the garden, I could even smell his hostility. Whatever happened, it would be impossible for Harry to live in my house.

That night, again sleep would not come. Not only was I torn by my sentiments against Harry, but I also anticipated his treachery the next day. What would I do if he forced Ava to go with him? At my slightest hint of attack, he could paralyze me. Damn him! I wished he were dead.

What if Dick and Minie were poorly received and were not permitted to return? Clearly Harry, living with Ava here or in the garden, was an obstacle to my happiness.

Edam, Harry—what kind of creature had I become? Of what further crimes was I capable? But crime meant a breach of law, and in terms of law, Harry had no status as a person. As a non-person, a thing interfering with the natural course of my days, he was an excrescence to be plucked out of existence. He would not be missed, surely not by Ava.

Yes, Harry was a troublesome object. His odd little life, devoid of moral scruples, made it senseless to consider him evil; that would assign him a worth the ground people themselves could scarcely accord each other. Thus, if Harry were a thing, I could exterminate him. Then why did anger cling to me like flesh until it sprouted the hairs of my skin? Was this not proof of my self-delusion, proof that Harry was not a thing but a person, endowed with the right to good and evil, in which I shared and should be judged?

At last it was morning, and the time had come for departure. The others awaited me in the kitchen. Dick and Minie seemed excited. I wished that Harry would change his mind and go with them in a gesture of friend-ship—didn't he owe them that?—but he would never leave Ava with me.

And the penknife? Harry might have offered it for the couple's protection. Why had he hidden it without men-tioning it to me? Outdoors, I peered at the rhododendron bush where he had placed it. I could not see it there.

The weather was cool. The wind hurtled through the branches, loosening the leaves. I would have to rake them up before they damaged the lawn. The grass needed cutting. Another week of neglect and the place would look deserted.

As anticipated, Harry made a last effort to persuade Ava. She shook her head and refused to take another step. There, damn you! I thought. She's told you off, you inflated vegetable.

"She wants to stay," I observed pleasantly.

"We will see."

"If the others are friendly," promised Dick, "we will come back and tell you."

"We will wait for you," Harry replied.

"Good luck!" I called to Dick and Minie as they began their trek across the patio.

Ava was shivering. "I am cold." Opening the door, I let her and Harry into the house but could not bring myself to enter. I lingered on the step, hands in pockets, surveying the woods. The grass rake leaned against the shingles beside me. I seized it and went to my front lawn. I kept raking the leaves.

By lunchtime the house was quiet. Ava had climbed into a corner of the sofa where she sat in miserable silence. Harry paced back and forth, pretending not to notice me. I smiled at Ava who smiled back wanly.

"Dick should be here soon," I reassured her.

Harry said nothing; Ava looked unhappy again. His anxiety apparently mounting, Harry told me, "Let us see the garden from your room."

"It would not be wise," I cautioned perversely. "Be patient." Although he remained silent, I imagined that scent of attack about him.

As I prepared my lunch, he came to the kitchen and stationed himself by the screen door, where he trotted restlessly back and forth. Ignoring him, I finished my tuna fish sandwich. Afterwards in the living room, I sat on the sofa with Ava. I smiled and put out my hand, communicating as best I could with my eyes.

Ava stared; then she smiled, and nodded. She touched my hand lightly, attempting to convey something, a longing, an affection she dared not express. She smiled and nodded again, as if to say, yes, I meant that, when suddenly she looked away.

"Come here!" snapped Harry. Ava's obedience infuriated me. "He is back!"

I hurried to the door where Dick was standing on the mat. "Good news!" he proclaimed, rushing inside. We all went into the living room and sat on the rug.

"Tell us!" said Harry. "Tell us everything."

"It is better than we hoped!" Dick exclaimed.

"How? How is it better?" questioned Harry impatiently.

"They want us to return!"

"Do they know—about Edam?"

"They suspect. It does not seem to matter."

"Do they know—our part of it?"

"I said they suspect, but it does not matter."

Harry frowned. "We must be sure."

"You worry too much," Dick said complacently. "Minie is there. If you had seen them—"

"I did not see them!" snapped Harry.

"You should have," blurted Dick. "Then you would be certain." Harry scowled.

"They say they need you."

"Oh?"

"To lead them."

"Yes," he agreed, his dourness lifting. "They do need me."

"I said Ava was with you. Do you know what they offer?"

"I am waiting to hear!" Harry sounded ready to shake the information out of him.

"They want you both to live in Edam's house."

"Aha!" Harry drew out the vowel musically and turned to Ava. "Did you hear?"

She remained silent.

"Well?"

She shook her head.

"We will accept," he announced, exasperated.

Ava responded in a whisper so soft that I heard it like my own wish.

"No," she said. She opened her mouth as if to say more and closed it quickly.

"I will not argue." Harry's voice trembled.

"I cannot go."

"Cannot?"

"I do not want to go," she said firmly.

Dick became fidgety and rose to leave. "Minie is waiting for me."

"We will come," Harry promised. "Expect us."

Dick seemed embarrassed. "If you do —"

"We will!"

I accompanied Dick to the kitchen and opened the door.

"Harry may stay with you," he said.

"Perhaps."

He gave me a quizzical look and disappeared. From

the kitchen, I could hear Harry's raised voice. Back in the living room, I saw that Ava had climbed into her favorite corner of the sofa while Harry marched comically back and forth on the coffee table.

"You made me appear foolish!" he scolded. "I—the next leader—I am very upset! Disappointed. I have given you so much—nearly my life, yes, risked my life for you."

"I did not ask you to," Ava said evenly.

"That is a lie! You told me—"

"I told you to do nothing."

"You said you were unhappy. That was enough for me. You knew that."

"How could I know what you would do?"

Harry paused, his fists taut at his sides. "You dare to say that now—"

I darted to the sofa and sat down. "Come, now," I said.

Harry shifted his ire. "Leave us alone!"

"I could be of some help," I insisted coolly.

"We do not need you!"

"You are rude to him!" Ava told Harry. "Joseph is our friend. Do not be ungrateful."

"Ungrateful!" he sneered. "You are not the one to use that word."

"There seems to be a question," I said coldly, "of whether Ava should go with you. Why would you compel her? If she doesn't wish to go, she will be perfectly safe here with me."

Harry ran to the edge of the coffee table and shook his fist at me. "That is what you want! I knew it. I know everything! Do not doubt that. Ava belongs to me! Remember that. She knows," he turned cunningly to her, "she knows what I can do. If I return without her, the others will blame her for what happened. And," he thrust at me, "they will blame you. Neither of you would enjoy such a life. It would be no life at all!"

"Animal!" screamed Ava. "Crow! Weed!" She covered her face with her hands.

"You are a worthy successor to Edam," I told him. "He was predictable, but you are treacherous."

"I will leave this house!" he shouted. "Now! We are not welcome here." He turned to Ava. "Come!"

She raised her head, frightened. "No!"

"Leave her alone!" I warned.

"You do not command me. I command. You will see!"

"Please!" Ava moaned. "No more. I agree."

"Ha!" he exulted.

"I will go with you tomorrow."

"There is no reason to stay," he said, confused.

"I will go tomorrow," she repeated wearily.

Harry relented, trading the skirmish for the battle. "All right. We will go in the morning."

He hopped down from the coffee table. "Ava," he said with a newly brisk manner, "you must come for a walk."

"I am so tired." She shot a pleading glance at me. What was I to do?

"Ava!"

Limply she slid off the sofa and faced him. Taking her firmly by the arm, he led her away.

The idea that he might now force her to the garden sent me outdoors. From the back step, I observed them walking down the driveway. Harry jabbered continuously while I waited, ready to pursue them. They halted, obviously quarreling, then started back. Soon they reached the door and we went into the house.

Alone in the kitchen, I opened a can of spaghetti for my dinner and heated the contents in a small saucepan. My meals had become irregular and unbalanced, a fitting complement to my life. In a kettle I boiled water for instant coffee, another concession to an increasingly tasteless existence. Only one thing, one being could restore my world, my rightful joy: Ava. I had to rescue her.

I tossed the spaghetti onto a plate and began to eat standing up. The food tasted flat, the coffee flavorless; nothing was as it should have been. I scraped the remains of my dinner into the garbage pail, put the dishes into the sink, rinsed them off, and left them there unwashed.

A small sweet voice drifted up to me. "I came to say good night," said Ava, "and good-bye. Harry wants to start early. I—I will miss you."

"Maybe—you will stay," I whispered.

"Oh, if I could—!" Her voice dropped. "Help me," she said.

Harry appeared. "Saying farewell? Cheer up, Joseph. You may come and visit us in the garden. You will not see us every day, a man as busy as you," he sneered. "Of course, we have to set things in order, first. Right, Ava? And I want to thank you for your help. We appreciate it, don't we, Ava? Without you, we would not be where we are, or what we are. Yes, you have helped to make us what we are.

"We will leave early, so sleep well, Joseph, and good-bye. Until we meet again."

He left, Ava trudging dejectedly after. She hesitated, looked back once, and continued on to their room.

XII
Night

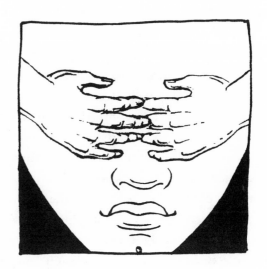

I sat in the kitchen, staring out the window at the gloomy rhododendrons that held their spearlike leaves poised in the darkness. An hour passed. I finished the cold coffee at the bottom of my cup. It would be good to sleep.

But I heard Harry's words again and again as they ran up and down my skin, nudging into little crevices, alerting me fully like some poisonous tonic. I washed the few dishes and quickly put them away. The kitchen in order, I turned off the light and walked softly to the storage closet near my room.

Carefully I opened the tackle box and removed a small, metal object. Behind my locked door, I placed it beside me on the bed, flicked on the bedside lamp, and took a book from the hanging shelf. Seated on the bed, I tried to read. After a few pages, I closed the volume and placed it on the night table as I struggled to compose myself.

No longer accustomed to intensity of feeling, I knew self-doubt would undo me. I held the penknife, my bounty from the tackle box. It felt heavier than the one I had given Harry. I pulled out the blade, tapped it lightly — still sharp! How many bloodworms, how many pale-armed squid had I cut to entice fish? How many struggling blowfish, who had dumbly swallowed the hook and the bait, whose mouths I had cut to retrieve their folly; or else I had cut the line and left the hook in them, piercing its way into their flesh?

Returning the folded knife to my pocket, I realized I must not question for a moment the necessity of killing Harry.

I recalled the little people wearing dolls' clothes, preening themselves and swaggering about the living room. One did not murder a doll. One broke it like a feather plucked from the imagination, nothing more.

Through the blind I saw that the garden was dark. My windows were closed and locked; I was locked in the room, box within box. Was the exterior all, imposed upon emptiness? I had had my fill of that. My fingers would seize what they wanted, one pair of hands in a world bristling with raptorial hands. Who from this world could censure me?

I remembered Emma, giggling that spring afternoon (had she been amused to fancy herself the predator?), while I seduced her from my friend. He had been studying — I was to escort her to an outdoor concert in his stead. We walked away from the concert and the village into the woods, through the marsh grass toward the bay. I had brought a blanket and she lay down — how small and fragile! Open-eyed, she laughed and I did, too, as I lay beside her, tall and strong in affection and longing. Recently I had shrunk a bit in height, I knew (I still measured myself occasionally against a pencil mark made long ago at the foot of the cellar stairs), the way some older people stoop as if expected to with age. I resolved to improve my posture and thought myself truly wicked, to be concerned with such triviality when I was literally bent upon killing.

I took the penknife from my pocket and opened the blade. If Harry were asleep, it would do the job well. And Ava: would she be asleep or awake? surprised? hopeful? It was time to begin. Suppose Harry were awake, sitting upright in bed, his hatred armed with a deadly spray? Yet I was propelled by my surging need. Once through the door, speed would be imperative. I suppressed the urge to urinate.

I removed my sandals and set them by the bed. Slowly, noiselessly, I turned the lock, then my doorknob, and stepped out, clutching the knife. Swiftly, I crossed the darkened hall. Putting my hand upon the knob, belatedly I thought Harry might have locked the door from the inside. I had an outside key, but it would make noise. Delay might betray me.

Turning the knob to the left, I eased the latch and pushed. The door was unlocked.

Both beds were occupied. A shaft of moonlight showed Ava sleeping beneath the window.

Harry huddled, worm-like, on the bed near the door. I knelt alongside him, lifted my arm, and struck, drawing the knife cleanly across his neck, feeling the bedspread beneath it. Harry's skin was soft clear through, like a mushroom. I felt no bone, saw no blood. The knife slashed a tear in the bedspread. I had used unnecessary force.

Harry made no sound. His head rolled a little toward me. His limbs moved suddenly in jerks and I panicked, striking wildly at them until they were severed. Panting, I wiped the perspiration from my forehead with the back of my hand.

I pulled down the bedspread and removed the pillow. A shiny object lay on the sheet. It was the missing penknife, its blade still extended.

I slipped off the pillowcase, thinking I should have brought an extra one (so much for impulsive acts and faulty preparation), replaced the pillow, and pulled up the bedspread. I lifted Harry's body and dropped it in, piece by piece, followed by the two knives. Ava stretched her legs as I glanced at the other bed. Had she been watching me? Behind her closed lids, was she crouching in horror?

I took the bundle and ran. Outside, the shovel I had used a few days before still rested against the shingles. I grabbed it and hurried along the grass bordering the driveway. Reaching the mound, I deposited the bundle and began plunging my shovel deeply into the sand until I struck something dull and stiff. Edam! But it was only a tree root.

Wary of attack, I peered sharply about. The impartial moonlight outlined me as clearly as the three cedars to my left, the lawn behind me, and the road.

I scooped out a last shovelful of sand. I knotted the pillowcase at the top and threw it in. Overwhelmed by my need to urinate, I wanted to drown the bundle triumphantly, but turned aside to make sure I would not pee into the grave. Then, my throat tightening, gasping for breath, the blood pounding in my head, I hastily piled the sand back and ran barefoot with the shovel over the jagged bluestones, aware now of the pain. I propped the shovel and entered, locking the door. It was over.

I felt no relief. I went to the bathroom, washed up, and still felt unclean. In pajamas, lying on my bed once more, I knew that somehow it had gone wrong. A moan quivered my lips. I heard my voice, unfamiliar, as if issuing from an anguished ventriloquist. A person's a person, no matter how small. My body sank and sank in an endless descent, unbroken by pity.

My God, I thought. I am crying.

✦ ✦ ✦

Someone spoke my name.

I looked up. Day was lightening the room. Ava sat on the bed, a few inches from my head. She reached over to touch my cheek.

"Are you all right?" she asked.

"Of course." I wondered what she observed in my face. "I heard a sound," she said.

"Oh?"

"I heard your voice."

"I'm fine."

"Joseph?"

"Yes."

"The other bed—in my room: it's empty."

She noticed the torn bedspread, I thought.

"Harry is gone." Again she paused for a reply. How could I lie to her? Terrify her with the truth? She might run away!

"Oh."

"Are you afraid?"

Puzzling question. "No. Certainly not."

"Joseph, I know—" Her voice faltered as I stared at her. "I know that Harry will not come back. I am glad. He was evil. Worse than Edam. Do you believe me?"

"Yes."

"I was afraid of him. He threatened me."

"How?"

"That knife—that terrible knife. He slept with it under his pillow. He loved it. He loved it best."

I sat up, facing her. "My poor Ava!"

"I hated him. I—I am so happy you—helped me."

She knew. She knew, and yet she had come.

"You—saw?"

"I saw you in my room. I knew you came to help me. I closed my eyes."

Was she lying? Had she seen everything? I neither cared nor wanted to know. "You are not angry?" I asked.

She smiled. "Never with you."

Her words came at me gently as a butterfly, brushing me with a delicate happiness.

"You are tired," she said.

"Yes."

"Sleep. You can sleep, now."

I thought: Don't go. The words would not be uttered.

"Do you wish me to stay?" A powerful offering, a sweet redemption.

"Yes."

She smiled. I turned on my side and drew her toward me. Still smiling, she slipped out of my hand and slid under the sheet. I kissed the top of her head. I could see the small imprint of her stretched-out body. Slowly, I pulled back the sheet.

Ava lay there voluptuously, her look inquisitive. As I moved my thumb delicately over her tipless breasts, she smiled again. My pleasure sent a familiar tingling down my spine and around my groin, and my shirt grew damp.

Gently I kissed Ava's face, her body incredibly soft and cool, her hands that touched me. A wave of joy burst upon me, lifting me into the sparkling air of my flesh.

XIII

The Beach

I awakened to a light stroking of my cheek. It was true: Ava was with me. I smiled at her and she laughed. "You have big teeth," she said.

"To bite you with."

She shrieked in mock terror and slid off the bed. I followed her into the kitchen and raised her to the table. "I wish I could help you," she said wistfully.

I busied myself with the coffee pot, then boiled an egg and made toast. As I sat buttering the bread I watched Ava's face. She seemed to study each gesture intently. How many years since anyone had attended my morning meal or even cared what I ate? I had rarely breakfasted with my son; Emma ate later with him before he left for school. She was usually cranky in the morning anyway, so that I preferred to eat in private, making my own coffee, leaving it hot for her to gulp down upon arising while I drove to work.

Her behavior was bearable, however, in the way that familiarity can be borne. My mother had been another matter—mounting her attentions upon me one day, withdrawing them the next, usually to favor my younger brother (a year my junior and asthmatic), and then withholding them forever when he died in an accident. I remembered his funeral, my father trying to console my mother, she with a furiously stricken face that assaulted us over the poor, crushed body in its closed casket. I thought of Edam, then, with surprising pain, as I imagined the horror of my brother's cut flesh after falling off his bicycle in front of a car. My mother retreated into a raging silence; my father veered away into his job. I thought of the dead: my parents, my brother, my wife, watchful, grieving in their caskets for their own losses, removed from concern for me into the permanence of our mutual isolation. Paradoxically, the prospect of my new happiness could no longer deny them access; they came tumbling out of their graves, the caskets flinging open to spill upon me the dire and anguished odors of their profusion.

I opened the window next to the table. When a breeze fluttered into the room, Ava shivered, and I lowered the sash.

"It is colder in the morning," she said.

"Yes. Autumn has begun."

She stared out the window. "When I first came to the garden, it was warm in the morning. Now it is not. I feel a strangeness on the breeze," she said dreamily. "The leaves tell it when they fall. Something will happen."

I was disturbed. "Nothing will happen. Not to you."

She smiled. "No. You will protect me. You are strong."

"Your garden friends wouldn't hurt you. And I doubt they'll miss Harry. They might welcome you back, if you want to go."

"I will never go there," she said fervently, "without you."

I took her hand. As I studied her, that dear little creature who wished only to please me, I grew eager to share with her more of my world. I would show her the bay, the ocean, the potato fields, even the town. We would continue the reading lessons and discuss my books and magazines. I expressed my plans.

"Yes!" she said to everything. How grateful I was for her enthusiasm.

"The clothes," I remarked, "are all yours."

"All of them?"

"Every one. Even the men's."

"Wonderful!" She stood on the table. Her mouth tapped my cheek like a wand. "May I try them now?"

I put her on the floor and she rushed into the living room. In a few minutes she emerged, wearing a blue dress.

"Do you like it?" she asked gaily.

"It's pretty."

She ran off and returned in a red skirt and white blouse. "Do you like it?"

"Very nice."

She hastened away. Soon she reappeared in a long satin gown. "This one?" she questioned hopefully.

"They are all fine," I answered, turning away. Suddenly, incalculably, she was grotesque.

Ava left the kitchen and came back, unclothed.

"Please pick me up." From the table she inquired, "What is wrong?"

"Nothing."

She lowered her head. "Joseph, I know how I—look to you. I thought you wanted me to wear the clothes—like the ladies in your magazines."

"You don't have to copy them. You are—different."

"I see." Her tone was sad. "It is hopeless. I am ugly."

"That's not true!"

"In the garden, I was like them. Here—" Her voice broke. "I cannot change myself."

"I don't want you to."

She sat wearily and her head drooped.

"I like you as you are," I insisted, alarmed, "not as a doll or a puppet. I was wrong about the clothes."

She stared, uncomprehending, as I tried to explain. "You are very dear to me," was all I could manage.

"Kind Joseph," she said quietly, "you pity me."

"No!"

"Yes, it is true. I am so small, like a speck on your life. And I have no hair on my head. Not one!" she added mournfully.

"I do not value hair so highly," I insisted, self-consciously patting the gray-black strands that thinly covered my scalp. "Perhaps we should say that I have ugly hair growing out of my head and that I am a giant. It would be just as true—or as false."

"You are good to me!" she exclaimed, jumping up to kiss me again on the cheek. "No one, no one is better than you."

Oak leaves were falling like petals on the driveway. I remembered a poem I had memorized when I was eighteen, a poem by e. e. cummings. In love for the first time,

I used to recite the words to the walls of my room, too shy to say them to the girl. I recalled her: a quick, light step through my youth, a backward glance over her shoulder to smile briefly and marvelously at me.

though i have closed myself as fingers,
you open always petal by petal myself as spring opens...
nobody, not even the rain, has such small hands

Stop! I told myself. Small hands, indeed! What has love poetry to do with Ava, the Creature of Ludicrous Size? You are dreaming. Wake up. Be prudent, practical, moderate, circumspect. Be reasonable. I imagined the message on a gigantic billboard:
WAKE UP AND BE REASONABLE!
"I'll take you for a drive," I said. I carried her out to the car and lifted her to the front seat. Moving without fear, I realized that the other garden people were ceasing to exist for me. With Ava, moreover, I had become invincible; they could not harm me. I supposed they would adjust to Harry's absence as casually as to Edam's. Dick had not seemed zealous to have him back, and the females were probably glad to be rid of Ava's troublesome charms.
We pulled out of the driveway. As we started down the road, I told Ava, "Someone might ask about him."
"Him?"
"Harry."
"Ah." Her mouth seemed to tighten. "I do not think so."
"But it's possible." I realized that I had become complacent.

"Then we will say we know nothing. He said he was returning to the garden one morning. He left before we were awake. Perhaps he was eaten on the way—by a dog. Or carried off by a sea gull. We could say we saw the sea gull. Or the dog." She grew pensive. "Which story is best?"

Her ingenuity startled me. A vision sped ahead on the road: I as puppet; Ava pulling the strings. "If we must lie," I said, "then let the lie be simple. The simplest lie is best."

"Yes."

"Let us say that Harry went outdoors early one morning. We did not see him leave. That is enough, I think."

"You are wise," she sighed, snuggling against me, "wise and strong. I am so happy." I wondered whether she had told Harry how wise and strong he was. Or Edam.

Longing for the unfettered sound of breakers, I drove straight to the ocean. At the foot of a narrow road lay the dunes. We were alone. From the back seat, I took a zippered bag lined with a small towel at the bottom. There Ava could hide, if necessary.

I tucked my companion into a large, inside pocket of my reversible jacket. Climbing the dune to view the shore, I saw a car approach. I transferred Ava to the bag and zipped it partly closed. Half-sliding, I hurried down the dune to the water.

"Joseph!" I heard her call from the bag. In my haste, I was swinging it freely with poor Ava careening around inside. I stopped, furious with myself for handling her so carelessly. My car still monopolized the parking area. The intruder had vanished.

"I'm so sorry, my dear," I murmured, removing her from the bag.

"I am all right. Please don't worry." Her concern was for me.

At the shoreline, the water mustered its force and hurled it forward, proud, profligate, reclaiming the sand, the broken shells and stones, casting up a solitary crab or fish.

I clasped Ava. "This is the sea."

She gazed outward, her eyes wide and tinged with a reflection of blue and green.

"Please let me walk."

"Stay near my feet," I cautioned. "The water is strong and deep. It can be treacherous."

"It is beautiful."

I put her on the sand. We walked together toward the breakers, stopping short of the foam left by the last wave. I sat down and took her into my lap. For awhile we were silent, looking toward the perfect rim of the horizon. The world lay connected, beyond the roaring moment, in a serene arc, within whose distant planes the mind, the heart could rest.

"I am so small," Ava remarked quietly, "too small for this world of yours. I do not belong in it. I am here by mistake."

I smiled. "I have thought that, too, about myself."

She was puzzled. "You? But it is all your size."

"To you, Ava, I am enormous. By myself, I feel trivial. The world itself is a tiny sphere, like a cinder in the universe. But with you I become—as you see me. Do you understand?"

"Yes. Sometimes, when I am with you, when I think of how I care for you and you for me, I am no longer an insect on your sleeve. I am—your size—a giant!"

I laughed. "And the two giants lived happily forever after."

"Forever after," she repeated seriously.

Glancing down at her smooth little head and over the water to the sky, hearing a gull and the silence, the very motion and stillness of space, I was thankful for that instant of life. Something singular was unfolding an unknown self upon an unknown road, as if I were being born again, endowed with a journey that was itself a glorious kingdom.

Yet I could not take that next step, the special word of praise. Locked within, it enclosed me. Like a door in which a key of trust had faltered before one last degree of turning. The turning had stopped. And so I could not speak the word of praise.

A late afternoon breeze blew up from the ocean. Ava shivered and I drew her toward me. "I feel cold," she said. "It's time to go." I put her into an inner pocket of my jacket, picked up the beach bag, and left. We had had our day at the beach.

XIV
Others

I sensed that something was wrong as soon as we entered the driveway. With Ava still resting in my jacket, I examined the mound of sand. Clearly I remembered flattening it to merge with the slight incline of the land at that point. Now there were several little mounds.

Could it have been an animal? Moles left linear patterns; raccoons were untidy; chipmunks and squirrels sought nuts in the woods. Ants? Armies of ants? Improbable here. Someone had been digging. When? On our way to the beach, I might have failed to notice the traces. Or else it had been done in our absence. Even a few minutes ago. Was somebody spying on us?

"I think the others have been searching," I told Ava. "I'll take you to the house. I must work here awhile."

"I can stay with you."

"Better not."

"Please, Joseph."

I gave in. Why maintain the public fiction of her innocence as if it absolved my guilt? As if, without a witness, there existed no crime?

I retrieved the shovel from its station by the kitchen door and went to the sand. I lifted Ava from my pocket, lowered her to the grass, and dug rapidly. Scrutinizing the sand unearthed my old suspicions.

What Ava had done no longer mattered, but what might she do? Did she really prefer me, and why did she require closeness, even now? How rough my hands must have felt on her skin!

I dug deeper, uncovering stones and roots. Had I delved this far last time? Then I felt a yielding, a fabric: the pillowcase. It was still knotted at the top. On one side, however, I saw a tear.

Ava was watching. Reticent (ashamed?), I kept the pillowcase out of sight in the hole. Reaching down, I opened the case at the tear, removed the penknives, and tossed them into the hole. I raised the pillowcase, flicking it inside out. A few goose feathers drifted to the ground. Harry's body had disappeared.

It might have decomposed without a trace. Or had an animal found it? Where was Edam's body? I ran to the house for my rake and carefully drew it through the sand. I dug again, more deeply, and found nothing.

The tear in the pillowcase was long and neat. An animal did not chew or use its paws that way. The fabric had been rent by hands, hands that had examined its contents and removed the dismembered body.

I raked the ground smooth again and stood immobilized. Finally I said, "The others have found what they sought. We may be in danger."

"I am not afraid."

Ava's calm disturbed me. I picked her up and we went back to the house. Inside, the familiar kitchen orderliness, the white, impersonal machines and ready coffee pot calmed me. I had not eaten lunch. With my companion deposited on the table I began to make dinner. While the canned hash sizzled in the pan and the coffee warmed, Ava sat patiently.

I ate, preoccupied and yearning guiltily for the peace of my solitary days. From the cabinet beside the refrigerator I took a bottle of Scotch and poured from it generously into a glass that I drained with a few, searing gulps. Relaxing, I further dulled my thoughts with the mechanics of chewing and swallowing.

Morbidity was foreign to my nature. Morose and lonely as I had felt, the question of surviving rarely occurred. Life was there, self-evidently a good, no matter how paltry it seemed at times. Good or bad, one went on—it was over soon enough, anyway. And with Ava (until now) I was more positive than I had been. I sipped my coffee.

"How do you feel?" she asked.

"Better. I was hungry."

"You are worried."

"Naturally I'm worried!" I replied impatiently. "Your friends may be plotting to kill us. This bothers me. In fact, I can't understand why it doesn't bother you."

"Sometimes it does," she said softly.

"Maybe you don't feel threatened. Maybe," I went on unkindly, "it's less dangerous for you."

She would not be provoked. "There is danger here for both of us."

"And the others are plotting—"

"Yes. I think they will try to kill us. They forgave Harry. He was one of them. But not you. And I am with you and share your guilt."

"For Edam, not Harry."

"For Edam and Harry."

"You should leave me, save yourself if you can," I said, watching her closely.

"No! I would not do that."

"We may be mistaken," I persisted. "Perhaps they are not angry with me about Harry. They may be glad."

She stared at me. "No," she said firmly. "They are not stones. They feel. They feel you have used one of them."

"Used?"

"Yes."

"But they use and abuse each other. What were you—any of you—to Edam or Harry? It's permissible, apparently, among yourselves."

"That is what they think." She paused. "Is it not the same in your world?"

"I suppose so. Yes."

"Everyone feeds upon his own garden, is that not so? An outsider is wrong because he is from outside, if he comes to feed. Do you not say," she went on, "that he does wrong?"

"We call it 'dog eat dog.'"

"The people become dogs?"

"In a way."

"You did not tell me dogs eat each other."

"They don't."

"I have seen dogs go down the road as friends."

"It's a saying—it refers to people."

"Then people are worse than dogs."

"They just follow their needs."

"It is the same in the garden," mused Ava. "Yes, that is why I want to be with you."

I was wary. "Perhaps I am like the rest."

"No!"

I stroked her shoulder. "Then I am not."

"You are fine, better than everyone," she said shyly.

I laughed, relenting. "I may be the worst of the lot."

"You are the best. Strongest and best."

"The strongest are best?"

"You do not understand." Her tone was subdued.

"Ava, I was teasing."

"My people have their strength. This is not what I mean. To me," she emphasized, "because you are kind and good, I think nothing can harm you. Nothing can harm me. I am in your jacket pocket. Do you understand?"

"Yes."

I wanted to say more, but that was all I could manage.

At night, as Ava lay cradled in my arm, I wondered what the ground people might do. I was prepared: the windows were closed and partly covered by screens. No odor could enter. As far as I knew, they had no other weapon against me. It was possible, barely possible that they would go away. If only they would disappear!

Dozing off, I heard a sound like rain that registered too sharply for raindrops or even hail. I sat up. The noise was focused at the gardenside window. Numbly, I recognized the sound of stones.

"What is it?" Ava whispered.

"Someone is throwing stones."

"They are doing it!"

"Yes."

"They want to break the glass."

"I think so."

"Ah."

Then silence. As we waited, Ava on the bed, I at the window, I heard my breathing and my hand trembled on the blind. It started again, first a few taps of pebbles, followed by the stones, larger now, coming fast and noisily, a barrage of stones clinking against the glass, shaking the window, pelting it into a clamor of resistance. I shuddered, hearing at last the unmistakable punctuation of a crack. I thought: Now they will do it, they will break through and the end will come.

They stopped. The night was passing slowly as I waited for them to begin again. But there were no more stones. Wearily I sat on the edge of the bed.

"It is over," said Ava.

"Are you sure?"

"Yes."

"Why did they stop?"

"I cannot tell."

"A few minutes more and they could have finished us off, or driven us out and attacked us outdoors. I don't understand it."

"I am so tired," said Ava.

"I will board up the window."

"If they wish they can try another."

"I suppose I could board them all. But I won't!" I added, enraged. "I won't lock us up, damn them! I wish they were dead. I'd like to kill every one of them."

Ava said nothing. I thought, God, I longed for them to grow, to be like me, now I want them dead. I thought: It is a war.

I lay back on the bed. Ava touched the moist corner of my eyelid. "A speck in my eye," I told her, rubbing it. She did not answer.

XV

A Moisture That Infuses

It was a gray day. I awoke early, unrefreshed, and went to the blinds. With defiant tugs I pulled them up. The wind rattled the panes of the front window, tearing innocuous rays of light into pallid shreds across the clouds. Leaves whirled over the grass, clustered in drifts, and moved again. Soon the lawn would be covered and the grass would die. Some of the trees were already bare, waving their victim branches in the wind.

Through the garden window, the enormous oak nearby held stubbornly to desiccated leaves. I saw no one. The garden seemed empty.

Returning to the bed, I lay down with Ava. She was so huddled that I could not see her face. But she must have felt my presence, for she stretched out and reached toward me. Shuddering, she opened her eyes.

"I am cold," she said.

"I'll turn up the heat." I went to the thermostat and shifted the indicator to seventy-nine degrees, activating the initial groan of the boiler. In bed once more, I watched Ava. Overnight, her expression had changed, though I could not tell precisely how.

She saw me staring at her. "I feel strange," she said.

"In what way?"

"Cold."

I tucked the blanket around her.

"The heat will come up soon. Does the blanket help?"

"I—I don't know."

I waited. "Feel a bit warmer, now?"

"No," she whispered. "I am so cold—inside."

"A chill," I murmured.

What could I possibly do for her? She did not eat or drink. How could I give her medicine? What kind? How much? Medicine might hurt her, might even kill her.

"Something is wrong with me," she said.

God! I thought. She's ill and I don't know what to do.

I kissed her forehead. It was cool. Her eyes looked somewhat dull. But what was it about her face?

And then I saw. Yes, that was it. Her face was no longer perfectly round. Her skin looked different. Could her color have darkened?

Her skin was no longer smooth; I saw it clearly, as if it had lost moisture and were beginning, almost imperceptibly, to dry up.

"What is wrong with me?" she asked fearfully.

"You are probably just tired."

"No. What do you truly think?"

"I don't know. How do you feel?"

"Cold—and stiff—is that the word? My legs are strange."

"Your arms?"

"My arms, also," she said, moving them awkwardly. "Oh, Joseph! I am afraid. I do not know what will happen."

Her distress terrified me. Hysteria choked me like phlegm.

"Stay in bed," I told her. "Rest, this morning."

"I want to be with you!"

"Please rest. For a little while."

I touched her head with my lips and went to the kitchen, where I put up some coffee, then rushed back to the bedroom.

"Are you all right?" I asked.

"Yes." She smiled faintly.

In the kitchen, distracted, I drank the coffee burning hot. I left the cup half-empty near the sink, and returned.

"How do you feel?"

She did not answer at once. "Have you eaten your meal?"

"Please tell me."

"I will be well. Eat. Come back when you have finished."

I withdrew obediently to the kitchen and attempted to eat a slice of bread and jam. I drank my coffee and hastened back.

Ava's eyes were closed. At first I was pleased that she was sleeping. Like the other creatures, however, she had no pulse or breathing to judge, and I feared she was dead. With icy fingers I tapped her lightly on the face and stroked her cheek. She fluttered her lids, smiled briefly into my anxious face, and became still.

Desiring to keep her awake, I was tormented by restraint. In a moment, fear would loose me to throw myself on the bed and frantically shake her into consciousness. But I would not disturb her rest. I tucked the blanket gently around her and tiptoed out. Her pain followed me; it filled the house.

I went to the front door and escaped to the front steps. Seated there, I clung to my knees, shivering, feeling restless and cold. I rose to examine the outdoor thermometer and saw that the temperature was nearly freezing. I went in to peer at Ava and lowered the blinds. She was still asleep; the house was warming up. Having raised the thermostat another couple of degrees, I went out again.

The oil truck came into the driveway on its monthly trip. I exchanged a few words with the oil man as he attached the hose to replenish our supply. When he left, I crossed the lawn, shuffling through the dead leaves, oblivious to the wind that struck my face. The road was empty.

I had no intention of hiding. All that mattered was Ava. Looking toward the garden I saw nothing, yet prudently kept my distance.

I cannot be alone again, I thought. Again I went in. Ava was resting; I was relieved that she had opened her eyes. "I will get up, now."

"Stay. Rest."

"I want to be with you." She strained to sit up.

"I'll stay right here," I promised. "But you must lie down."

"No. I must move. It is better for me."

I sat beside her, watching her face. "Would you like to look out the window?"

"Yes." She could not raise herself. "Carry me, please."

I picked her up tenderly and took her to the front window. Lacking vitality, she appeared more fragile than ever. "It is cold," she said.

"An early frost."

"I want to see the garden."

I took her to the other window and raised the blind. The ground was strewn with oak leaves, nothing more. "I think they are gone."

"Perhaps." She turned suddenly and clutched at my shirt. "Put me down."

Setting her on the bed, I was horrified to see her grimacing. "What is it?"

"The pain—" She twisted her body to one side.

"My God." I could not endure her suffering, my helplessness, and flung myself beside her. "Ava! Ava!" The movements stopped. Her face assumed its natural tranquillity.

"What do you feel?"

"Nothing," she said. She gave me a sad, pitying smile. "Do not be afraid."

"I want to help you. I would do anything—"

"I know."

"There must be a way."

She turned from me.

"Is there? Tell me. Please."

She paused. "There may be."

"What is it?"

"The garden—at night I could sleep there, covered by the earth. It might heal me."

"Let's go right away!"

"It is not time."

"Why?"

"You must accept that," she said softly. "Take me there tonight. Leave me there. It would be dangerous for you."

"And for you."

"I will be safe." She made a scratch of a smile.

"I cannot leave you." I thought: She is right, you are vulnerable, you may die there, in the night. The others may return and attack you, kill you on the ground as you sleep.

I will not leave her! I argued silently. You are a fool, I responded. Be sensible. Save yourself. You cannot save her.

I will be with her, protect her with my body and share her fate.

She looked at me as if she understood my decision. "Joseph, you are a good man." Then she closed her eyes.

As I lay with her, anguish engulfed us like a sea where her small body floated beyond my drowning fingers. Hours passed. As the room darkened, I grew impatient with hope.

"Ava," I called, rousing her. "We can go soon."

"I will go."

"No," I said firmly, "we will be together."

"It is cold there," she said.

"I have a sleeping bag."

Her voice was faint. "If you wish."

In the hall closet, I found the sleeping bag. Originally it had been mine; then my son used it on a Boy Scout camping trip. I remembered his enthusiasm, so rarely displayed, when he asked if we might camp together one Saturday night in the backyard. We made a tent with a sheet; he used the bag and I wrapped myself in a blanket.

Within an hour I felt damp and crawly, assaulted by a backache going into my legs. Finally I left the tent, he following, and I brought the sleeping bag, neatly folded, back to the house and into the closet.

When my son came to breakfast the next morning, he ate cornflakes with his mother who fussed over the possibilities of his having caught a cold; she, so terrified of illness, who had developed cancer but perversely died of pneumonia, almost easily as if, in slipping away from us one winter, she had performed a grotesque trick, preparing it all her maternal life for the day her son would graduate and move far away. Across country to California. Our son.

I clutched the sleeping bag to my chest. Then I threw it over my shoulder and entered the bedroom. Delicately, I picked up Ava and carried her in my arm.

The wind whipped the darkness about us, and I walked over the patio flagstones, dreading time. Hour by hour Ava had weakened. My concern for her life allowed none for my safety. I had no fear of death.

I dropped the sleeping bag in the center of the garden. Above, the long branch of the giant oak poised like a skeleton in the air. I put Ava down.

"Cover me with the earth," she said. While she lay on the ground, I broke some clumps of earth over her until at last she was hidden up to her neck. She smiled at me.

"I feel good," she said. I kissed her cheek. She closed her eyes and went to sleep.

I got into my bedding and reclined next to her. It was too cold to sleep. I kept thinking of the morning, wondering whether Ava would improve by then. I moved closer. The others might come. What would they do to her?

Would they hurt her? I was thinking only of Ava, and the idea gave me peace.

The stars were pale and scattered and the moon cast a timid brightness over the trees. Yet on that cold ground, in the desolate hours, I felt a profound warmth that sustained me. I wanted to tell Ava about it.

I thought: I will tell her in the morning. I was able to sleep fitfully, waking without fatigue. It was as if my self, having lain asleep nearly a lifetime beneath this very earth, were rising at this late season, defiant of frost, prodding me awake. There was a touch of joy in that.

She will recover, I thought, concentrating, trying to will her healing. I was about to doze off again. The sky began to lighten and the cold settled into an early morning stillness. The wind had abated. I imagined that the rustling I heard was a last shudder of air among the few dead leaves overhead.

Then it came down, only a whiff at first, like a wisp of memory, accumulating a volume of scent, acrid, unmistakable: the odor of attack.

I tried to grab Ava and escape. As I reached toward her, a wave of the smell hit me with paralyzing impact. Choking, half-blinded by smarting tears, I doubled up over the small mound be-side me. Each gasp seared my lungs until I tried to stop breathing.

Something struck my head and I looked up. Through my blurred vision I saw a dark object fall from the overhanging branch. Another fell, and then another, and then several at once like a dark storm. What was it?

I had been holding my breath, and now my lungs were bursting and I had to inhale. My breath seemed

less painful. I breathed again, and it was true: the air
was clearing.

I peered around me in horror. The ground writhed
with shriveling bodies, convulsed in soundless agonies:
the garden people. Their newly brownish color had cam-
ouflaged them among the branches. Now they were
fallen, contorting like giant worms.

"Ava!" I looked at her. "Not you!" I moaned. "Not
you!"

Her face had turned quite brown and striated, like
tree bark. Beneath the earth her body moved in irregular
jerks. I brushed away the soil revealing her in the same
violent spasms I observed in the rest. Glancing wildly
about, I saw that one by one the bodies were becoming
still. Her movements, too, were subsiding.

"Ava. Please!" Her eyelids fluttered and closed.
Could she hear me?

"I love you!" I cried out, as I had meant to tell her.

The only visible movement of her body was a steady
trembling, like the prelude to rigor mortis. I had seen
Emma like that. Even as I watched Ava, the shaking
diminished into an irregular tremor, barely perceptible.

I kissed her poor withered face, knowing that I kissed
a dead thing. Prostrate, I lay by her rigid body. I could
have placed my words, my self, like an amulet within her
stiffening fingers, to take with her—yesterday.

Now I was pain. I was nothing at all.

I stretched out, hoping for stiffness, for a last whiff of
that paralyzing scent that might draw me with her into
the ground. Hour after hour the sun advanced, dispens-
ing light without warmth. Nothing stirred.

Why was I still alive? Left behind?

The tiny bodies resembled twisted twigs that might have been loosened by a gust of wind in the oak tree. Stiff and aching, I sat up to survey the garden people, all of them past recognition.

I would bury them.

I walked back across the patio to retrieve my shovel and a small wooden box. In the middle of the garden I dug a hole deep enough for the container. I decided to place the other bodies in the pile of sand near the driveway. But Ava belonged with me. She would be there in the garden, outside my window, always.

I set the box near her. As my palm met her shoulder, I was sickened to feel it crumble in my hand. I tried to lift her, and her body disintegrated. Beneath the lightest pressure of my fingers, Ava became earth.

I tapped the other bodies, transforming them one by one into little mounds. Except for their shape, it was impossible to distinguish them from the rest of the soil.

Turning from the terrible scene, crying with rage and despair, I grabbed the handfuls of earth that had been Ava, dropped them into the box, and put the box into the hole. I covered it, tamping the ground firmly with the back of my shovel.

Then I scanned the tiny piles of earth scattered among the leaves and the bare ground. Lifting my shovel high, I brought it smashing down on them, flattening them into the dead leaves and the soil. Briefly I viewed the garden and went for my rake.

I raked the ground smooth. Free of mounds, stones, leaves, twigs, roots, free of everything but earth, death, memory. Here lay the unfelt, unspent grief, coming out of the trees, the bushes, the shadows, rising from the ground—all that I could not show or feel for Emma, for Jason going away, for Jason. Saying his name at last revived his presence and the sorrow it bore me, sorrow that came leaping out of the closed album of the past, free of the soil in which it had mildewed, to stand now beside me, filling the space around me with remorse and impossible longing. All the losses I had ever experienced came surging over me, transformed into ocean waves that were drowning me in the soil of my garden. I recalled my visit to the ocean with Ava, who lay at my feet in an unmarked grave. I put a stick into the soil. Something beautiful should be planted there.

I picked up the rake again and thought: I am buried alive in a small box, with handfuls of earth. The rest of me lies scattered, in the garden, the sand, everywhere. Nowhere. I am nothing but earth and air, a moisture that infuses and escapes, the memory of something that one cold night was springing from the ground to touch me. A sob shook me at the thought of it, the harrowing, irretrievable loss of it.

But was it the end? Could anything hold the perfection of finality, like the period terminating a sentence? Life wasn't neat, wasn't an orderly assembling of puzzle pieces; it was sloppy, overlapping, a mess. Even with the last piece, the whole would remain the question. The garden people died; they survived in my recollections. They might return—as flowers, insects, birds, in the forms of clouds or the sounds of summer. Life continued. Ah, but let one specific thing come back—even one sound! Let it be Ava's voice—if I could only have that—even as part of the morning light, the breeze, the birds at dawn or dusk, a robin, an owl, or a nightingale—her voice.

If it were true that our bodies changed and exchanged atoms, that there was a constant exchange of atoms in the universe and we were physically, not just metaphysically (as most religions believed) part of one another—the good and the bad, horror and holiness, timeless in time, in such a universe we might forgive one another, and the unity itself was love.

Could Jason forgive me? Had I pushed him too hard, onward into business? Hadn't it been more my choice than his? Pushed him away from me into Emma's anxious arms? Was that why he seemed to be groping toward this and that, trying to discover a choice of his own? A sentence floated up, beached lightly as foam. "You're not listening, Dad." What was the lost context? No matter. "You're not listening." A dismal memory—and legacy— for us both. Why should he listen to me now?

It was hard to listen, of course, when one was so damn tired! My feet ached with the memory as I leaned on the rake. I had been busy closing off the importunate world of dailiness, a world baffling me into a retreat that shut it up and out.

Jason! I realized that he had not been bumbling along, but seeking. Would he find a clump of golden fleece? A skein of it having started as what—an umbilicus? A golden umbilicus! How terrible it must have been for him when Emma died, the one who had loved him most, the one who thought him perfect. While I had grieved angrily that she had left behind no resolution of our differences, had dumped our estrangement into the ground that held her, he had grieved truly, and alone. Now, as I mourned for Ava, I understood his terrible loss.

I picked up my discarded sleeping bag, leaned the rake against a shingle, and walked back slowly to the house. I paused to shake the bag free of soil, then carried it on my arm. Alone again, solitude was no longer the simple condition of my life: It had become a tomb. I sat on the back steps. A towhee rustled the dry leaves in search of bugs. I sat numbly in the cold, the sleeping bag draped across my jeans.

My stomach began to ache and would no longer be ignored: I had not eaten since the previous morning. As I rose to enter the house, clutching the empty bag, I felt the need to speak to someone, to release my secret that, even as I stood, was drawing me earthward. Who would care about my story, not because it was fantastic, but because it concerned me? Who, perhaps by the ordinary ministries of the magic that had stirred me, might encourage my survival?

I thought of Jason, compressed by the years into greeting cards, small checks on his birthday and at Christmas, sent more out fear of Emma's ghostly retribution than with love. I could not simply call him up (we spoke only in response to my checks and at Thanksgiving)—that would be as strange as my story itself.

My hand was on the doorknob. I could neither enter nor remove my fingers. Then I felt the gentle pressure of Ava's hand, guiding mine. She was with me, enhancing my life, moving my fingers as she had moved my heart.

I would write a letter to my son.

Turning the knob slowly, I went in.